M000028045

# Special Thanks

Special thanks to our daughter Leticia Kreider, for her many hours assisting us in writing and rewriting this book; Lou Ann Good, for her research, editing and excellent writing assistance; Sarah Sauder, for her project oversight and design; Merle Shenk, for his pages of contributions; Steve Prokopchak and Peter Bunton, for reading the manuscript and offering valuable insights; Kim Zimmerman, for her research and recommendations, and Nancy Leatherman, for her eye for detail in proof-reading. We are so thankful to the Lord for each of you.

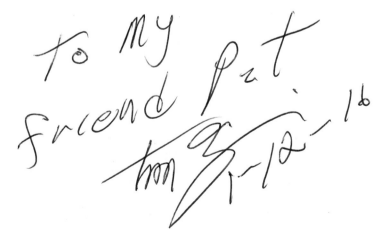

I go east, but he is not there.
I go west, but I cannot find him.
I do not see him in the north, for he is hidden.
I look to the south, but he is concealed.
But he knows where I am going.
And when he tests me,
I will come out as pure as gold.

(Job 23:8-10 NLT)

# CONTENTS

# How to Use This Resource

## Personal study

Read from start to finish and receive personal revelation. Learn spiritual truths to help yourself and others.

- Each reading includes questions for personal reflection and room to journal at the end of the book.
- Each chapter has a key verse to memorize.

## Daily devotional

Eight weeks of daily readings with corresponding questions for personal reflection and journaling.

- Each chapter is divided into seven sections for weekly use.
- Each day includes reflection questions and space to journal.

## Mentoring relationship

Questions can be answered and life applications discussed when this book is used as a one-on-one discipling/mentoring tool.

- A spiritual mentor can easily take a person they are mentoring through these short Bible study lessons and use the reflection questions for dialogue about what is learned.
- Study each day's entry or an entire chapter at a time.

## Small group study

Study in a small group setting or in a class or Bible study group.

- The teacher teaches the material using the outline provided at the end of the book. Everyone in the group reads the chapter and discusses the questions together.

# Introduction

So many times we desperately want to know what God wants us to do, but He seems to be silent. We wonder if God is hiding from us or if He is displeased or angry.

In this book we examine times of God's silences and various barriers that block God's voice. We learn from the Scriptures what God is really doing in our lives behind the scenes when we are in the midst of confusion. We also reveal some of our own struggles with God's silences and the tremendous breakthroughs we experienced from these various life lessons.

*When God Seems Silent* is the first book in a new series we are writing called *The Time Is Now!* This series is based on the scripture: "The right time is now" from 2 Corinthians 6:2 (NCV). When is the best time to make a change in your life? The time is now!

About twenty years ago, I (Larry) wrote *The Biblical Foundation Series*, a 12-book series used to help both new and mature believers to understand the basic foundations of the Christian life. These books sold hundreds of thousands of copies and are translated in many languages throughout the world. Often I have been asked, "Are there any more books written with this same basic format that can be used for personal study and as a tool in a spiritual parenting or mentoring relationship?"

This new series, *The Time Is Now!* is the answer to that question.

This book can be used in the following ways:

- Personal Study
- A Daily Two-Month Devotional
- A Mentoring Relationship
- Small Group Study

*When God Seems Silent* will help you discover *"The Time Is Now!"* to listen and hear God's voice, and to find God's purposes during seasons of confusion and darkness in your life. It will also give you practical spiritual insights to help others who are facing similar challenges.

God bless you as you read each page. Our prayer is that you will hear our Father God speak encouragement and life to you today through the Scriptures.

Larry and LaVerne Kreider

# CHAPTER 1

# When God Seems to Stop Speaking

**KEY MEMORY VERSE**

Never will I leave you;
Never will I forsake you.

Hebrews 13:5

## When It All Falls Apart

I wanted to quit. Feeling like a complete failure in ministry and leadership, I felt hopeless and misunderstood. I was serving as the senior pastor of a mega church that had started with twenty-five people only ten years earlier.

LaVerne and I knew we had clearly heard God's voice to start this church, and we remembered the many times we had heard God speak to us since surrendering our lives to Him. But at this time, God seemed to be silent, distant and nowhere to be found. In fact, it felt like the more we cried out to God for help, the more silent He became.

We were in desperate need of help.

We were in the midst of personality conflicts and differing opinions regarding the future vision for our church. It felt as though everything was crumbling down around us. We confessed all of our sins and faults, but our circumstances stayed the same. We received personal deliverance ministry, yet it did not break the silence. Even as we tried to claim His promises, God did not seem to be helping us. We were tired. Silence remained.

I begged God to help me bring unity among our fraying relationships with some of our church leaders, but things only grew worse. God continued to be silent. I believed God had called me to pastor and lead this church, but after growing opposition, I doubted God's call on my life. After all, if God had placed me in leadership, I should be able to hear Him and bring resolution. But resolution evaded me. Not only was I feeling like a failure in church leadership but also as a leader in my home. When I looked into LaVerne's eyes, I saw the hurt she was feeling from the rejection of others. In my children, I saw the pain of not knowing why some of their daddy's friends no longer spoke well of him.

If I was the husband and father God intended me to be, I was sure I should be able to come up with solutions that would heal fractured relationships and shelter my wife and children from hurt. But I couldn't. Where was God when I needed him most? Why didn't He answer? According to the Word of God, He wants His people to live in unity. Obviously, since unity wasn't happening, I was to blame. It certainly could not be God's fault.

> Why did the God that I love and serve so faithfully, leave me during these dark hours in my life?

If God was speaking to me during this season, I was failing to hear Him because of the hurt, failure and fear that smothered His voice. Instead, the voice of the accuser grew stronger in condemning me for everything that was wrong. I was convinced that all God had done in my life was ending in shambles. Why did the God who I love and serve so faithfully leave me during these dark hours in my life?

But the truth is this: God didn't leave me. He promises in Hebrews 13:5, "Never will I leave you; Never will I forsake you." He really means it. He was with me constantly, and working in ways I did not comprehend at the time. It was during the silence that I gained many invaluable lessons. I learned that even when we are convinced He is silent, He is working deep beneath the surface of our lives.

**REFLECTION**
*Describe a time when your life seemed to fall apart.*

Have you experienced the silence of God? Are you finding it hard to hear God speak to you in this season of your life? We have good news for you! God may be doing his deepest work in your life during this time. He may be teaching you to listen to His voice in ways you have not yet experienced. Read on as we learn together how we can hear His voice when He seems to be silent. The time is now.

## There Is Hope!

**DAY 2**

If you feel devastated by God's silence, there is hope for you! God is working beneath the surface of your life. We do not say this just to make you feel better. We know it because it is confirmed in God's Word, and we have experienced it personally. The Bible records example after example of how God worked beneath the surface of people's lives.

During my darkest hour, I read the story of Joseph in Genesis. For years it appears that God was silent when he allowed Joseph to be sold into slavery by his brothers. When Potiphar's wife accused Joseph of rape, he was thrown into prison for years. A prison inmate promised to advocate Joseph's release in exchange for Joseph's help, but even the ex-con went back on his promise. Why didn't God protect Joseph from his jealous brothers? Why didn't God defend Joseph from the lies of Potiphar's wife? Why did God allow Joseph to remain in prison? God seemed to remain silent.

Today, when we read the ending of Joseph's story, we know that God was preparing something far greater in Joseph's life than offering him temporary help. God may not have been speaking in the way Joseph wanted at the moment, but God was orchestrating a better answer. It was a plan that elevated Joseph to second in command in Egypt! This plan saved Joseph's family from starving to death and eventually reconciled him with his brothers. (You can read the story in Genesis, chapters 37 through 50).

Joseph's story demonstrates God's faithfulness and gives us hope. In Genesis 45:8, Joseph told his brothers, "So then, it was not you who sent me here, but God."

> God used and continues to use the season of our greatest pain to impact our lives and ministry for good.

In our own circumstances, LaVerne and I identified with Joseph. We came to see that our circumstances were not necessarily the result of people or even Satan attacking us. God used and continues to use the season of our greatest pain to impact our lives and ministry for good. Through the grace of God, we did not quit believing in God, nor did we quit Christian leadership.

Although LaVerne and I would have been content to remain as pastors, God had other plans. Our church began to start other churches. We were appointed to lead a leadership team that gives spiritual oversight and provides mentoring to pastors and spouses in our family of churches. This network grew into an international family of almost three hundred churches in twenty different nations. LaVerne and I went on to experience the joy, peace and fruitful ministry that surpassed our initial prayers.

Today, we understand the pain people feel as they struggle with the silence of God. We empathize with those in leadership positions who need hope when their world seems to be falling apart. We can speak from experience.

God is working in your life even if you can't hear Him clearly. We are confident because God's Word teaches us that He works during the silent seasons of our lives. Joseph told his brothers, "You intended to harm me, but God intended it for good to accomplish what is now being done, the saving of many lives" (Genesis 50:20).

This book contains faith-building stories about believers in Christ from throughout the world. These believers

**REFLECTION**

*Are you wavering in faith because you cannot hear God speaking?*

discovered that God redeemed their darkest hours for good. We believe that you, too, will discover God is busy working in ways you cannot see at the moment.

## The Bamboo Tree Principle

DAY 3

In Thailand, a farmer plants a bamboo seedling but will not see any growth on the surface the first year. He patiently continues to water and tend to the seedling during the next three years. Suddenly, in the fifth year, the bamboo tree begins to grow. In fact, it rapidly shoots up two-and-a-half feet each day, for six weeks, until it reaches about ninety feet.

Although growth cannot be seen with the human eye during the beginning years, the tree develops a root system that is many miles long beneath the surface. During those first four years, the foundation is established to provide for the significant growth that eventually occurs.

The bamboo tree is an example from nature of how God often works in our lives. During the season when I (Larry) thought God was silent, He was weeding out my dependence on the approval of others' opinions and thoughts about me. I needed to learn to obey God and know that His love is enough to sustain me. The rejection I felt from fellow leaders stung. I really loved them, and I wanted them to affirm me and to believe in me. God knew that I needed to learn to receive my significance and security from Him, not from those around me.

I read in the scriptures that Jesus said, "As the Father has loved me, so I also love you" (John 15:9). That scriptural truth was life changing for me. I began to understand that I was loved by God and it became more than head knowledge. That truth became ingrained in my heart.

> During the season when I thought God was silent, He was weeding out my dependence on the approval of others' opinions and thoughts about me.

In years to come, I discovered that many Christians struggle with feeling insecure in God's love for them. A middle-aged man told me that he felt he would never amount to anything, because he had heard his father speak negative words over him as a child. He allowed those lies to influence his life, rather than the voice of the heavenly Father who says, "I love you, and I am pleased with you" (John 3:17).

I have prayed this scripture over many who wept as they received a revelation of their heavenly Father's love. This is a love that cannot be earned, but only received by faith. There is nothing that you can ever do to get God to love you more. There is nothing you can ever do to get Him to love you less. Our heavenly Father loves you, just because He loves you! (I John 3:1). I pray that God's love for you permeates deep into your soul.

When I was growing up, my parents grew perennial flowers called chrysanthemums, which become dormant and completely disappear during the winter months. With the right garden conditions, spring sunshine and rain bring vibrant growth. Some gardeners wanted massive plantings of chrysanthemums, but others wanted only a few to intersperse among other plantings. If they did not plant them in the right space, the chrysanthemums did not reproduce. Damage done from other aggressive perennials can choke out chrysanthemums just as much as weeds do. For example, if customers planted them near vinca vine, as the plants spread and intermingled, the vinca vine would choke the chrysanthemums. Both of those plants are attractive and useful in their places but toxic to each other when not pruned by gardeners.

In our lives, we may be thriving in a job or ministry or in our family, but our focus may crowd out other areas that God wants to develop. During the seasons of our life when God seems to redirect us, we often cannot hear or see God at work. The reality is that He is laying a root system within us that will produce abundant growth in fulfilling His purposes. He is a good God, a great father, and He knows what He is doing in and through us.

**REFLECTION**

*Reflect on your life. Can you see areas where God may be weeding out your dependence upon others so that you depend more upon Him?*

## An Unfamiliar Form

During some of the darkest days of my life, I (Larry) couldn't recognize Jesus. I was begging God to fix my circumstances and I wanted His supernatural intervention to bring unity to our church so that everything could proceed smoothly.

To my dismay, many in leadership left to serve in other places, and in retrospect, I cannot blame them. I had much to learn about healthy leadership. I begged God to intervene. I bargained and pled. I fought to fix things. I felt like the disciples must have felt after their Lord was crucified. Things had neither turned out the way they wanted, nor the way they were sure God had promised. Their hopes, purposes and dreams came crashing down around them.

In Luke 24:13-35, two of Jesus' disciples were walking along the road to Emmaus when Jesus joined them. The disciples were distraught as they discussed all that had transpired in the previous days. How could it have happened that the disciples did not even recognize the person they longed to see when He joined them and entered into conversation with them?

Perhaps the disciples were so immersed in the details of the dark events of the previous days, so they could not hear clearly. However, I think there is a good possibility that the disciples did not see Jesus because they did not expect to see Him. He appeared to them in an unfamiliar form, at an unexpected time, and their ears remained closed.

Looking back, I was so immersed in the details of the darkness, that I could not hear God's voice clearly. God was appearing to me in an unexpected form and working in my life in an unfamiliar way.

I was accustomed to praying for people to forgive each other and seeing resolution. Despite my prayers, I was not seeing the good things I expected to see. God was good, right? Therefore, I reasoned, God had nothing to do with the darkness that descended on my life in the form of disunity. But my understanding of His working within me was limited.

It was during this season that I learned how to "see" beyond my circumstances. The disciples walking on the road to Emmaus recognized Jesus when He

> I begged God to intervene. I bargained and plead. I fought to fix things.

gave thanks for the meal they were about to eat. "When he was at the table, he took bread, gave thanks, broke it and began to give it to them. Then their eyes were opened and they recognized him" (Luke 24:30, 31). When we give thanks, we open the door to see Jesus in our everyday lives.

I resolved to give thanks for all God had done in my life and to follow Him. I promised to obey God's call to continue to serve as the senior pastor of the church even though I did not feel qualified. The good news is that God reminded me that He had called me and that He would enable me. He brought a wonderful team of leaders around us who encouraged me to continue on with the vision God had placed in my heart more than ten years earlier.

Today, I know I have been created for His purposes. I know I am walking in the role He has placed me. I am no longer a pastor of a local church, but I am privileged to be a pastor to pastors in many nations throughout the world. Without experiencing that season, I do not know where I would be today. During my season of silence, the Lord showed me the areas in which I needed growth and prepared me for the days ahead.

**REFLECTION**

*Do you think it is possible that God is speaking in your silence? If so, how?*

## Beyond the Circumstances

DAY 5

The truth of God's Word must become more real than the emotions we feel. Focus on the truth of God's revealed Word in the Bible. His Word speaks life into our silence.

Our friend Janice told us of a time when she was experiencing a time of God's silence. Janice and her husband were Christians who were happy that their children had grown up to serve the Lord. One day their son began dating a woman who was not living for God.

Janice and her husband pointed out the many inconsistent values this woman portrayed compared to the Word of God. For a time their son broke off the relationship, and then suddenly he married her. His new wife knew her husband's family disapproved of their relationship, so she cut off ties with them and demanded her new husband do the same.

> By focusing on the voice of God's Word, we will eventually hear God speaking like He promises.

Janice and her husband were devastated. Within weeks, the marriage began to unravel because the woman was living an immoral lifestyle. The son attempted a reconciliation and through his wife's demands, moved with her to another state. Although the son and his wife no longer lived nearby, Janice and her husband were aware the couple were not involved in a church and appeared to be falling into a deeper, ungodly lifestyle.

Heaviness enveloped Janice. Why hadn't God answered their prayers for their son? Why had God allowed their son to make an ungodly decision? Now his life seemed ruined forever. Eventually Janice realized her prayers were filled with complaints, anguish and tears. She couldn't sense God working and didn't foresee how God could ever redeem the situation. But by faith, Janice arose every morning and said, "Nothing is too difficult for God. He is calling my son and his wife to surrender to Jesus. He is working. God is able to do amazingly above what I can ever ask or think" (Ephesians 3:20). She began to give thanks by confessing the promises found in the word of God.

Janice repeated these words and similar promises many times throughout her day. Often tears ran down her cheeks because she did not feel like God was answering. God seemed so far removed from the situation. He seemed to be silent, but Janice persisted because the Word of God says, "Nothing is too difficult for God" (Luke 1:37).

Within six months, Janice got a phone call from her son. He told her he was involved in a church and had recommitted his life to the Lord. He was still with his wife, but she refused to be involved in the church.

Janice and her husband continued to pray. A few weeks later, the son's wife committed her life to God. She called Janice and her husband and asked them to come for a visit. Within minutes of their arrival, the son's wife confessed many wrongdoings and asked for forgiveness. Her transformation is one of the most dramatic Janice had ever witnessed.

Do you see how Satan used the circumstances to discourage Janice? For a time, Janice allowed Satan's voice to drown out God's voice and He seemed to be silent. By faith, Janice learned to hear God in the silence by refusing to listen to other voices and choosing to believe the truth of God's Word. Janice focused on God's voice by proclaiming

His promises and giving thanks. Out of this obedience, she came to see that absolutely nothing is too difficult for God.

That same power is available to all of us. God's solution may not happen in six months or even a year. It

**REFLECTION**
*How are your circumstances drowning out God's voice?*

may be shorter or it may be much longer, but by focusing on the voice of God's Word, we will eventually hear God speaking like He promises. The results may be different than we expected, but we can trust Him. Even in the midst of feeling darkness all around us, He is working.

## The Proper Voice

We are all in a lifetime walk with the Creator of the universe and learning to hear His voice is a skill to be honed over time. Our God tells us to ask, seek and knock, and the Bible promises that He will open the door. God will reveal Himself to those who humbly seek Him. God is infinitely amazing, wise and creative. He does not limit Himself to speaking in the same ways all the time.

God is a little unpredictable. This is illustrated well with Aslan, the lion, in *The Chronicles of Narnia*. Remember Mr. Beaver's warning to the children: "One day you'll see him and another you won't. He doesn't like being tied down—and of course he has other countries to attend to. It's quite all right. He'll often drop in. Only you mustn't press him. He's wild, you know. Not like a tame lion."[1]

We must remember that God is God—and we are not! At times, instead of hearing His voice, we may be hearing our own voice. The decisions that we make may originate from our belief systems and mix into our personal feelings and desires.

I (LaVerne) have learned that sometimes we confuse our own desires with the voice of the Lord. Often our soul (thoughts, will and emotions) wants something so badly that we confuse it with hearing from God. This can especially happen during the silent times. We must be very careful if we are hearing something that primarily caters to our own comforts and desires.

> The words spoken over us from a very early age often become the things we believe about ourselves.

God speaks in order to accomplish His will, not ours. We quiet our own voice by dying to self. As we surrender to Him in our hearts, we take up our cross daily and follow Christ (Luke 9:23). We will then begin to hear the voice of God more clearly, not through our own self-effort, but by genuinely surrendering to Him.

We need to be careful to not confuse the voice of others for the voice of God. These voices are not to be confused with those who give us godly counsel, but these are the voices we hear deep inside by persons who try to sell us their products or philosophies. They are the subconscious voices we have collected and experienced over time. Whenever these thoughts and opinions distort the Word of God, we are told to have them demolished (2 Corinthians 10:5).

Our past experiences often mold us and sometimes in a detrimental way. The words spoken over us from a very early age often become the things we believe about ourselves. If these beliefs are in disagreement with God's truth, they distort our ability to hear God's voice clearly.

There are times that we can confuse God's voice with the voice of the enemy. The devil can quote scripture out of context, and he can use spiritual sounding language to confuse, entrap and derail us. He wants to get us to question God's character and turn away from him. How often have you decided to get serious about studying the scriptures and a voice reminds you that you are hungry? Tell the devil the same thing Jesus told him when he was hungry: Human beings cannot live on bread alone, but need every word that God speaks (Matthew 4:4).

As Christians, our desire is to hear and obey the voice of God speaking to our spirit. Psalm 46:10 invites us to "be still and know that I am God."

**REFLECTION**
*Why must we be careful to discern the voices vying for our attention?*

God might seem silent, but He is certainly speaking. He is teaching us to listen for the voice of truth.

## The Sun Is Still Shining

The sun was shining brightly when I (Larry) recently flew into the Harrisburg International Airport in Pennsylvania. When the plane pierced through the clouds to land, I could no longer see the sun because it was raining. From my perspective on the ground, the sky appeared dark. However, the clouds formed only a thin layer between me and the sun I had witnessed a few minutes beforehand.

Our friend Diane Omondi, from Nairobi Kenya, explains the irony of this perspective by saying, "On a rainy day, we may say, 'the sun is not shining today.' The sun is not shining? The sun, the unimaginable huge, unfathomably hot ball of blazing fire is *not shining*?

"How quick we are to limit life to our own perspective and to minimize God. Our perspective of Him may be like our perspective of the sun. We might say that God is good because my life is good. He has blessed me—so He is good! Yes, but from that vantage point, do you believe He is also good in the midst of the storms—in the darkest of nights? For even in the night, the sun is still shining. When we can see God at work even in our crisis, it brings us to a place of brokenness. This is not a bad thing! When we know that we cannot fix ourselves, we recognize we need Him desperately."

Rick Warren, author of the *Purpose Driven Life*, said that the year his wife was diagnosed with cancer was both the toughest and the best year of his life. He described life by saying; "I believe that it's kind of like two rails on a railroad track and at all times you have something good and something bad in your life. No matter how good things are in your life, there is always something bad that needs to be worked on. And no matter how bad things are in your life, there is always something good you can thank God for."

When we know that we cannot fix ourselves, we recognize we need Him desperately.

Rick's description challenges us to choose whether we will focus on the dark and negative aspects of our life or on the areas where the sun is shining. It might seem impossible to concentrate on God's goodness in the bleakness of the moment. When the fear of "what-ifs" blind us from seeing anything good, we question God's power and sovereignty. Let's ask our God to open our eyes to see the good things we are missing, to awaken and illuminate our spirit, and to fill us with an awareness of His presence.

Habakkuk 3:17-19 states: "Though the fig tree does not bud and there are no grapes in the vines, though the olive crop fails and the fields produce no food, though there are no sheep in the pen and no cattle in the stalls, yet I will rejoice in the Lord, I will be joyful in God my Savior. The Sovereign Lord is my strength, he makes my feet like the feet of a deer, and He enables me to go on the heights."

*29*

This verse reminds me of Laura. Her life seemed to be filled with one catastrophe after another, which she constantly repeated to friends. One day, she realized her words brought more attention to Satan rather than God's power. Conscious of her own negative words and the power they invoked, she stopped repeating negative happenings to friends. Instead, by faith, she verbally expressed the promises of God's care. Within weeks, God began working in astounding ways, and Laura found it easy to rejoice in the Lord.

Paul the apostle says in Ephesians 2:6, "that we are seated with Him in heavenly places." This position gives us the proper perspective regardless of what is happening around us.

**REFLECTION**

*Have you been tempted to believe that the sun is not shining because your life isn't being blessed in the way you desire?*

God is a supernatural God who loves to work in our lives. Remember, when He is silent, the night seems dark, and the clouds seem heavy, but the sun is still shining brightly above the clouds. Let us continue to be aware of that sun!

*27/min . To grasp rent*

# CHAPTER 2

# Seasons

# A Season for All Things

Do you feel as if your life is on hold? Do your dreams feel unfulfilled and fading? You are not alone. God has not forgotten your dreams. He is working behind the scenes in ways you do not see. God sees a beautiful diamond inside each of us, but it takes time for Him to remove the impurities in our lives so that we can reflect Jesus. Sometimes the refining process feels as if it's taking too long for a dream to be fulfilled, but God is as much concerned about the process as He is about the end result. Many times we miss what God is trying to teach us in the process because we are focused on wanting instant gratification.

Life is filled with seasons. The Bible says, "As long as the earth remains, there will be seasons" (Genesis 8:22). We would never think of swimming in a lake during our cold Pennsylvanian winters. In the summertime, our snow shovel is put away until the winter season piles snow on our driveway. God appoints seasons of preparation for us, and seasons when our dreams come to pass. Fulfillment of our dreams is dependent on God's timing.

Regardless of what you are going through, it is just for a season. If you are in an exciting spring season in your life, family, ministry or business, make the most of a time filled with fresh vision and blessing. If you are in a summer season of hard work and harvest, relish the growth! If you find yourself in a fall or winter season, when life seems to be fading or requires a cold drudge through the wilderness, keep trusting in the One who created all seasons for a purpose. Don't waste the season. What you learn in the dark will help you live in the light. God says, "I will give you hidden treasures, riches stored in secret places" (Isaiah 45: 3).

Ecclesiastes 3:1 and 11 clearly states: "For everything there is a season, a time for every activity under heaven. . . Yet God has made everything beautiful for its own time." Find something of beauty in the time and season you are in and remember, it is only for a season. You will never have that exact season again and regardless of the season you are in right now; it is just for a season. If you allow it, God will use it to prepare you for your future.

> Find something of beauty in the time and season you are in, and remember, it is only for a season.

The biblical character Esther went through a hard winter season as an orphaned child, but she was taken in by her kind cousin, Mordecai, and entered into a spring season. She was then chosen to be prepared to become the wife of the king of Persia, and eventually, she became the queen. The Lord had been preparing her for years to be in the right place at the right time, so that when the evil Haman tried to wipe out all of God's people, Esther was at a place of influence to stop his hideous plan. Mordecai asked his cousin Esther, "Who knows but that you have come into the Kingdom for such a time as this"? (Esther 4:14). You have also come into the Kingdom for such a time as this. Don't waste your season—God has great plans for you!

As I (Larry) look back over my life, it has gone by so fast! During my first fifteen years, I was simply learning about life. During the next fifteen years, I became totally committed to Jesus and learned about youth ministry, business, marriage, family and making disciples. The next fifteen years, I served as senior pastor of DOVE Christian Fellowship in Pennsylvania, where I learned about servant leadership. This prepared me for the following fifteen years, where I served with an amazing team of international leaders who helped start churches on six continents. Everything the Lord does through us in our present season helps prepare the way for our next season and also gives us the opportunity to help prepare the next generation for their future. Now, at age 63, I have been asking the Lord what He has for me in the next fifteen years of my life.

**REFLECTION**
*Which season do you feel you are in at this time?*

God reminds us that even in difficulties, as Jeremiah 29:11 says, "His plans for you are for good, to give you a future and a hope." But remember, God is committed first and foremost to His divine process of refining us and making sure that we reflect His Son, Jesus.

# His Perfect Time

So often, during times when God seems to be silent, He is teaching us to wait until the timing is right. Our God is teaching us endurance.

Hebrews 10:36 says it well: "For you have need of endurance, so that after you have done the will of God, you may receive the promise."

Merle Shenk, my friend and pastor in South Africa, recalls, "When my wife became pregnant with our first child, we were extremely excited. We told everyone the good news. The idea that I would be a dad for the first time felt unreal! Despite all the excitement, we still had another eight months to go before we could see our little girl."

Sometimes we obey God and are confidant and excited. We know our actions will bear fruit. While we are waiting for the fruit to come, we can become discouraged. At times we can become downright impatient.

There is no better picture of endurance than that of a soon-to-be mother during the eighth and ninth months of pregnancy. She endures discomfort and fatigue before ultimately receiving the promise of new life. God has His perfect timing, which requires the mother to wait regardless of how impatient she feels. Likewise if we are asking God for new direction in order to avoid endurance, God may seem silent.

A Christian businessman wanted to make money investing in financial institutions. Lured by the average yearly return of investment, he deposited a substantial portion of his money in a certain fund. He had grandiose dreams of becoming wealthy quickly and after a few months, he checked up on his investment. In shock, he realized that the value of his investment had not increased one cent! In fact it had decreased because of the initial brokerage fees. Despondent, he waited a few more months and when his investment was just above breaking even in profit, he heard of another fund that claimed an even more impressive return on investment. He hastily withdrew his money and put it in the new fund. Once again, he lost money due to paying fees. After some time, he did not think his money was earning enough, so he invested in a different market sector. Then a financial setback hit the market sector in which he had invested. He did not feel his money was safe, so he frantically withdrew it. He continued to deposit and withdraw his money from various funds again and again over the next several years, trying to catch the next upturn in the market and praying that God would bless his next investment. Ironically, if he had left his money in the initial investment from his first year, he would have been far ahead financially. He needed to learn to endure minor setbacks in order to receive the long-term financial return.

> There is no better picture of endurance than that of a soon-to-be mother during the eighth and ninth months of pregnancy.

As mentioned in Hebrews 10:36 there is a time between doing the will of God and receiving His promise. During that time, we need endurance, and if we approach God asking for a new direction, He usually does not give one. God is not moved by our impatience. Sometimes people claim to be hearing God when they jump from one activity, church, or significant relationship to another. Sadly, they never seem to receive the promise in these areas until they set their heart to endure in a place of obedience.

**REFLECTION**

*Is there an area of your life where you need to exercise patience?*

Leo Tolstoy said, "Patience is waiting. Not passively waiting. That is laziness. But to keep going when the going is hard and slow—that is patience." Patience does not mean a lack of doing, but it is full of action in your heart! Let's set our eyes on Him as we run this race before us. As the Apostle Paul told the Ephesians, "You have need of endurance. . . ." Therefore hold on, be patient, and trust in His perfect timing.

*Start 12-29-14*

**DAY 3**

# The Power of Thankfulness

On Thanksgiving Day, Charlie Brown's dog, Snoopy, was sitting in his doghouse grumbling to himself. Everyone was in the house eating mashed potatoes, turkey filling, and other scrumptious food, while he was stuck with his dog biscuits. Another thought then dawned on him. He said, "Come to think of it, I am thankful that I was not born a turkey!"

Like Snoopy, I have learned a few things about giving thanks.

Being thankful is a decision. We do not give thanks because we feel like it. We choose to give thanks because it is the correct thing to do. Colossians 3:15 says, "And let the peace that comes from Christ rule in your hearts. For as members of one body you are called to live in peace. And always be thankful."

> If we grumble instead of giving thanks, we are saying, "If I were God, I would not do it this way."

We give thanks because God is always good. No matter what we are going through in our lives, this holds true. Just as Snoopy realized, it could always be much worse! If we grumble instead of giving thanks, we are saying, "If I were God, I would not do it this way." We should remember that He is God and we are not!

We have found giving thanks to be the most effective way to find God's will for our lives. The Bible tells us to "give thanks in all circumstances, this is the will of God in Christ" (1 Thessalonians 5:18). Ungrateful people find it hard to accept God's will and purposes in their lives.

Giving thanks opens the door for God to show up in our lives. Before Jesus and his disciples saw the miracle of the 5,000 being fed, Jesus gave thanks for the few loaves and fish he had. The result? Fish sandwiches for 5,000 and twelve basketfuls left over!

Giving thanks gives us the right posture. When we have a heart full of gratefulness, it positions us to recognize the voice of God more quickly. The disciples on the road to Emmaus were holding a conversation with Jesus but only recognized Him as Jesus after He thanked the Heavenly Father for the food before them.

We visited Rwanda a few years after the genocide of a half million people who had been slaughtered by their countrymen. We were amazed by what we saw among those who had lost loved ones. They chose to give thanks in the midst of their grief. Some of the survivors even visited the local prison to share Christ with those who had killed their family members. Despite great pain, the survivors' decisions to choose forgiveness and thankfulness changed the nation of Rwanda.

Thankfulness will change our lives, too.

Did you notice what the verse in 1 Thessalonians 5:18 says to us? "Give thanks in *all* circumstances." So even when God seems silent, the Bible instructs us to give thanks. This is not because the God we serve is a harsh taskmaster, asking us to do things that are too difficult. It is because He knows the power and freedom that thankfulness brings to our lives! The story of Job is a beautiful example. Job kept an attitude of praise, even in the face of turmoil and

## REFLECTION

*In what areas of giving thanks do you need most to improve?*

death: "The Lord gave and the Lord has taken away; may the name of the Lord be praised" (Job 1:21).

Let's make a concentrated effort to meet with the Lord and to place ourselves in a position to hear Him through a thankful heart. The results will surely amaze you!

## Keep Your Eyes on the Prize

DAY 4

We are in a spiritual war that causes a battlefield in our minds. The devil knows that if he can get us to focus on failing, fear, poverty, disease or our negative circumstances, we will become defeated and depressed.

Nick Vujicic was born without limbs, but went on to accomplish amazing feats for which he is often featured in the international media. In his book, *Unstoppable: The Incredible Power of Faith in Action*, Nick Vujicic shares his upbeat attitude and confidence in God. Nick's faith in God was deeply challenged in his earlier years. He writes of losing faith and becoming suicidal by focusing on what he could not do rather than on what he could. "I lost hope in the future because my vision was limited to what I could see instead of opening myself to what was possible—and even impossible."[1]

Nick went on to say, "My lack of limbs wasn't the problem; my lack of faith and hope triggered my despair.... Instead of seeing myself as enabled, I saw myself as disabled....I yearned to be what I was not."

Nick's confident faith was rekindled as he studied the account in John 9:3 of a man born blind and how God worked though him to display His glory. Nick surrendered his life in full to God's strength. Since then, Nick has taken God's message to more than twenty countries and spoken to millions, encouraging them to surrender their lives in full to God's strength.

Like Nick, we often think God is silent because we focus on the circumstances that cause us to suffer. We want God to change our circumstances, not our attitude. God is more interested in refining our attitudes than in providing a life of ease. Ironically, when we surrender our circumstances to God and commit ourselves to trust him, the communication with God often opens the blockage to hearing His voice. Instead of listening to the enemy's lies, we need to pray, "Lord, I believe what your Word says about me. I know I am loved by my heavenly father."

> We often think God is silent because we focus on the circumstances that cause us to suffer. We want God to change our circumstances, not our attitude.

A big, tall toy on a heavy base can be found in some department stores. When you push it over, it always pops back up. That's the way God wants us to be when we fall—pop back up because we declare with confidence, "I will not listen to the lies of the devil. If I fall, I will get up in Jesus' name, and move on with my God."

A favorite verse of ours is Philippians 3:14, "Brothers and sisters, I do not consider myself yet to have taken hold of it. But one thing I do: Forgetting what is behind and straining toward what is ahead, I press on toward the goal to win the prize for which God has called me heavenward in Christ Jesus. All of us, then, who are mature should take such a view of things. And if on some point you think differently, that too God will make clear to you."

A fellow believer in Lancaster County, Pennsylvania says it well. "Times of being plowed and planted are not fun or glorious, but they do achieve a glory from God that far outweighs the pain." As it says in 2 Corinthians 4:17, "For our present troubles are small and won't last very long. Yet they produce for us a glory that vastly outweighs them and will last forever." In the same way, a long-distance runner may have many moments of wanting to give up, but he knows his momentary affliction will seem small compared to the adrenalin rush of crossing the finish line.

**REFLECTION**

*Where is your focus when things go wrong? How do you respond?*

In moments of despair and silence, it can be difficult not to focus on the seeming failure. But we are called, as sons and daughters of God through Christ, to place our focus heavenward. Keep your eyes on the prize

# When We Receive Bad News

Sometimes God seems to be silent after we receive bad news because the events are so opposite of what we interpret as God's goodness.

When medical tests disclosed that our friend Keith Yoder, president of Teaching the Word Ministries, had cancer, the threat of death disrupted his mind. Multitudes of prayer by friends did not result in healing during the ensuing months. Keith could have been discouraged by this unanswered prayer. Instead, he immersed himself in the meaning of Apostle Paul's testimony: "Whether I live or die, my existence is securely linked to Christ. Christ is the source of my life whether on earth or in heaven—now and always" (Romans 14:8).

The surety of this position refreshed Keith's mind, sustained his peace and focused his destiny. Keith said that during subsequent months, he got to the point that he rarely thought about cancer or even prayed about it. He says, "I had been transformed by renewing my mind with the Word of God." Keith eventually had surgery and five years later, his relationship with Christ witnesses to that eternal truth that Christ is the source of his life.

Keith's experience confirms that sometimes God doesn't answer our initial pleas for healing in the way we prefer. Consequently, we often chalk up the lack of a miraculous healing to God being silent. As in Keith's case, God worked to enable him to gain an eternal perspective, one that transformed his life: "For to me, to live is Christ, and to die is gain" (Philippians 1:21).

Where does your source lie? It is when we receive bad news that this question is tested. In his book *If God is Good*, Randy Alcorn writes, "When you feel God's silence, or think of him absent, look at Christ, the lamb silent before the shearers (Acts 8:32 NLT). He shouts to us without opening his mouth, 'I do care. Don't you see the blood, bruises and scars? Whatever you may think, never doubt that I care for you.'"[1]

> Many throughout the history of the church have called times of God's silence "the dark night of the soul."

Many throughout the history of the church have called times of God's silence "the dark night of the soul." It is a time of feeling completely alone, often in the midst of circumstances beyond our control. Yet they learned that these were often the times of God's deepest work in their lives.

Although it may feel like it, we are not alone. A pastor in Pennsylvania had a daughter in the ICU for eighteen days, hovering between life and death. Her kidneys had failed and doctors mainly gave them continual bad news and little hope. They immediately reached out to family and friends all over the world and asked them to pray. After one week, something happened to them without any rational explanation: their fear and anxiety lifted. Although their daughter's condition had not improved, their emotional and spiritual well-being had greatly improved. It was as if God whispered, "I know what you are going through. Trust me. We will make it through together."

The pastor recalls, "We did. My daughter was given a new kidney. But the greatest comfort we received was that the Messiah understands our sufferings, is acquainted with our grief, and afflicted as we are." Our pain and suffering may not make sense, but God still stands with us amidst it.

Many times, what we interpret as silence, God intends for us to grasp new concepts in His Word. We receive grace from

## REFLECTION
*Give an example of a time that you received bad news. What was your response?*

Him to sense His presence in ways we have yet to experience. Our God is good, and we can trust him.

# Learning from Jesus and His Disciples

DAY 6

We can learn a lot about God's seeming silence from Jesus and his relationship with his disciples.

Jesus' disciples were in trouble. They were told to feed over 5,000 people and all they had were a few loaves of bread and a few fish. Jesus blessed what they had and his disciples watched the loaves and fish supernaturally multiply right before their eyes. It was amazing! Everybody ate and they had twelve baskets of food left over!

Then Jesus insisted that his disciples get back into the boat and cross to the other side of the lake, while he sent the people home. It wasn't long until the disciples were far from land and in trouble once again. A strong wind had risen, and they were fighting heavy waves. Where was Jesus when they needed him? He seemed nowhere to be found.

> Only after she relinquished her questioning to God did she find peace.

About three o'clock in the morning, Jesus came toward them, and he was walking on the water. When the disciples saw him walking on the water, they were terrified. But Jesus spoke to them at once. "Don't be afraid," he said. "Take courage. I am here" (Matthew 14:27 NLT).

Within mere hours they had forgotten the miracle of feeding the 5,000. They focused on their circumstances, rather than on thanking and blessing God for what they had seen him do in the past, who He is, and for what He could do.

Jesus had to remind his disciples again in three short powerful statements, and he is reminding you and me with these same words today. Regardless of what we are facing at the moment, He is saying to each of us: "Don't be afraid. Take courage. I am here!"

Jesus faced God's silence on the cross when He said, "My father, why have you forsaken me?" Because Jesus took our sins upon himself on the cross, Father God had to distance himself from His son for a short season. Jesus completely understands what we walk through when we find God to be silent. He is telling us: "Don't be afraid. Take courage. I am here!"

In her book, *Light in my Darkest Night*, Catherine Marshall tells of her struggle to hear God after the death of a grandchild. She said, "It's the complete lack of response that confounds me. I've never ever lived in this kind of vacuum before. I talk, I pray. Nothing. For most of my life I've felt God's presence . . . no more. He's gone from my life."[1]

Her turmoil continued for months as she demanded answers from God. She struggled to make sense out of His seeming callousness to her petitions. Only after she relinquished her questioning to God did she find peace. She went on to say, "When life hands us situations we cannot understand, we have two choices. We can wallow in misery, separated from God. Or we can tell Him, "I need you and your presence in my life more than I need understanding. I choose You, Lord. I trust You to give me understanding and an answer to all my why's? —only if and when you choose."

**REFLECTION**

*Jesus made three powerful statements. What were they?*

Catherine had learned to relinquish everything to God; the good, bad, and the ugly. Then he met her. He calls us to do the same. This takes courage and understanding and we must listen to the words of our Savior, Jesus, and trust Him. So do not be afraid. Take courage. He is with you!

# Living in the Present

It seems like everywhere we turn, we find myself talking to someone who feels as if they are in the "land in-between." They know God has something for them in the next season, but find themselves waiting, and God seems to be silent.

Recently I (LaVerne) read a quote that helped me put it all in perspective. Although we are not sure who originally said this, it is certainly worth repeating: "Instead of praying, 'God what do you want me to do next,' ask, 'God, what do you want me to do while I am right here.' Direction from God is not just for your next big move. He has a purpose in placing you where you are right now. Begin to understand God's purposes for your life by discovering what He wants you to do now." God says a similar thing. "Give thanks in all circumstances, for this is the will of God for you in Christ Jesus" (1 Thessalonians 5:17).

One of the tricks of the enemy, aimed at trying to keep us from being fulfilled, is to try to tempt us to live in the past. If that doesn't work, the enemy will tempt us to be overly concerned about our future. God wants us to live to the fullest in the present and allow Him to reign in the midst of our problems. Matthew 6:33-34 tells us, "But seek first his kingdom and his righteousness, and all these things will be given to you as well. Therefore do not worry about tomorrow, for tomorrow will worry about itself. Each day has enough trouble of its own."

We appreciate the words of hymn writer John Newton when he said, "We can easily manage if we will only take, each day, the burden appointed to it. But the load will be too heavy for us if we carry yesterday's burden over again today, and then add the burden of the morrow before we are required to bear it."

Do not allow the past to steal your present, nor the uncertainty of the future to steal your joy. Every problem that we have is an opportunity for a miracle or new door to be opened. As you read through the Bible, you'll find that every miracle was preceded by a problem. The Red Sea parted because the children of Israel had a problem—they had to flee the pursuing Egyptians. Jesus fed the five thousand because there was a problem—the people were hungry. The blind man was healed because he had a problem—he could not see. God desires to use you today as an instrument of His miraculous power.

> Direction from God is not just for your next big move. He has a purpose in placing you where you are right now.

Alexander Bell, the inventor of the telephone, said, "When one door closes another door opens; but we so often look so long and so regretfully upon the closed door, that we do not see the ones which open for us." Let's not miss today's opportunity to experience a miracle because we are focusing too much on the past or on the future.

It is time to open our eyes, see beyond the obvious, and expect a miracle.

One of our friends said he spent a lot of time looking backward, wishing he could undo decisions that he regretted. Feeling as if he was a failure and had made too many mistakes, he wondered what might have been had he done "this" or "that."

"What a waste of time and energy," he says. "I have come to see that floundering over past mistakes is really a lack of trust in God—a lack of trust in His grace and forgiveness. God can redeem mistakes and weave both good and bad choices into a beautiful design to honor Him. Making mistakes is humbling but it helps me have empathy for others. I realized my need to depend on God and to trust him to work all things for good. His love and acceptance do not depend on my performance of perfection."

**REFLECTION**
*What does it mean to live in the "land in between?"*

God will lead us to new things, but for today, let's ask our God for His eyes to see what He is doing around us now. Then, we will not miss our God-given opportunities for today.

# CHAPTER 3

# Taking Baby Steps

**KEY MEMORY VERSE**

The steps of a good man are
ordered by the Lord.

Psalm 37:23

# Baby Steps

Remember the movie *What About Bob?* In it a therapy patient, who fears everything and anything, is initially advised by his therapist to take "baby steps" to learn how to function normally. The comical story takes us through many of Bob's antics as he learns to take those first, small steps.

When you take one small step of faith and God opens a door, then you can take another step. If He closes the door, then you back off. Try another direction or wait awhile; but always keep praying and step out again.

Even Jesus' parents had to make adjustments in direction until they had it right. An angel of the Lord appeared to Joseph in a dream and told him to take baby Jesus back to Israel. Joseph headed in that direction; but on the way, he was frightened to hear that the new king wanted to kill Jesus. Then in another dream, Joseph was warned not to go to Judea, so they went to Galilee instead and lived in Nazareth (Matthew 2:19-23). Joseph and Mary were not sure what steps they should take, but they took one step at a time in obedience to God as He opened up new doors and pathways.

The Lord knows that He could overwhelm us by revealing His whole plan at once. It's so big that we might be frightened and not take the first step. Consequently, He leads us one step at a time so that we can handle it. Psalm 37:23 says, "The steps of a good man are ordered by the Lord."

Some of God's people spend their lives in so much fear of making a mistake that they never do anything. There are times when it is much better to do something rather than continue to do nothing. Without faith it is impossible to please God (Hebrews 11:6). Obviously, there may be other times when waiting is better than any action for the sake of it.

Sometimes when we take baby steps in faith, God may seem to be silent. This can be the best time to train ourselves to be in a position to hear Him better. After the silence is broken, we may be more prepared to step out in obedience than ever before. The writer of Hebrews tells us that we can train ourselves to recognize the voice of God above all the other voices we hear. "Solid food is for mature people who have been trained to know right from wrong" (Hebrews 5:14). Learning to hear the Lord clearly takes time and practice.

> Some of God's people spend their lives in so much fear of making a mistake that they never do anything.

God is constantly speaking to us, but we must tune in to the right frequency to hear Him clearly. Radio, television, and cell phone signals surround us continually, but we need the proper receiver to hear these signals or see the pictures projected properly. Likewise, we must place ourselves in an appropriate and listening posture to hear God's voice.

Samuel, a mighty prophet in the Bible, learned as a small boy to hear the Lord's voice, but it was a process. He didn't recognize the voice of God when first spoken to him. At first, God's voice sounded like the prophet Eli. Perhaps God first spoke to Samuel in a voice that was familiar to him, so that he would not be frightened. We believe God often speaks through a voice that we recognize. Sometimes it may sound like our own voice or thoughts, while at other times, God may speak through someone we know. Even if it is unclear at first, God's voice will always lead to His peace inside of us.

**REFLECTION**
*Can you think of any baby steps the Lord may be leading you to take in faith?*

In this way, we must learn to posture ourselves to listen and discern for His voice. Don't worry if you feel like a modern-day Samuel, who does not recognize God's voice right away; you will learn in time! Listen and take steps forward, no matter how small those steps may be. Keep listening and stepping out in faith!

## The God of the Second Chance

**DAY 2**

Do you ever feel as if you made too many mistakes? That the Lord probably will not speak to you clearly as in the past? That He can never really use you effectively again? We have good news for you. Our God is the God of the second chance. Look at Jonah. After running from

God and being swallowed by a great fish, the Bible states, "Then the word of the Lord came to Jonah a second time" (Jonah 3:1). God gave Noah a second chance and God often does the same for us.

Now is the time to place all of our trust in Him. We must be convinced that if God doesn't show up, it's all over. But He will show up! God has a "track record" of using those who feel as if they cannot do the job. Remember, man looks at the outward appearance, but God looks at the heart (1 Samuel 16:7). When our heart is at the right place—in complete submission to Him—it is amazing what the Lord can do to prepare and equip us for the responsibilities that lie ahead, regardless of our past track record or feelings of insecurity.

> A feeling of "I can't do it" is a common thread that runs through the life of almost every individual who has been called by the Lord to serve regardless of their capacity.

When Jeremiah was a young man, he told the Lord, "'Ah, Sovereign Lord, I do not know how to speak; I am only a child.' But the Lord said to Jeremiah; 'Do not say, "I am only a child." You must go to everyone I send you to and say whatever I command you. Do not be afraid of them, for I am with you and will rescue you'" (Jeremiah 1:6-8).

A feeling of "I can't do it" is a common thread that runs through the life of almost every individual who has been called by the Lord to serve regardless of their capacity. But this is the type of person the Lord will use—those who are completely dependent on Him.

No matter what your task is in life, the Lord promises to be with you and help you. He is the God of the second chance. Let's not waste our mistakes but learn from them by purposing in our hearts not to repeat mistakes. Philippians 1:6 says, "For I am confident of this very thing, that He who began a good work in you will perfect it until the day of Christ Jesus." Don't allow the fear of missing the mark stop you from taking hold of another opportunity the Lord gives you to try again. This could be your door to breakthrough!

The first step to having a breakthrough is to admit we need one. Second, we must believe a breakthrough is God's agenda for us. That is why reading scriptural accounts of breakthroughs and hearing testimonies of God's faithfulness are so important. They build our faith. And third, when we pray for breakthrough in accordance with God's Word, we can know it is on its way. We persevere and refuse to quit until we experience the breakthrough.

**REFLECTION**

*What is the first step to having a breakthrough in your life?*

Daniel fasted and prayed for twenty-one days until the angel Gabriel came and instructed him (Daniel 9). Praise God Daniel did not quit before he experienced breakthrough.

There are many examples in the world of those who did not quit after making mistakes. The great baseball player Babe Ruth struck out almost twice as often as he hit a home run. In twenty-one years, Ruth hit 714 home runs but struck out 1,330 times. He said, "Never let the fear of striking out keep you from taking a swing." How much more should we as believers in Christ refuse to quit. God is on our side!

Remember, the God who has begun the good work in our lives will see us through until completion (Philippians 1:6). We can trust Him! So get back up and refuse to look back. Today is a new day. Today is a day of second chances.

# The Fear of the Lord

A few years ago I (LaVerne) began to understand in a new way the biblical truth of "the fear of the Lord." The Bible tells us, "The fear of the Lord is the beginning of wisdom" (Proverbs. 9:10). In other words, if we have a deep reverence and love for God, we will gain wisdom. We are also told in Proverbs 8:13; "To fear the Lord is to hate evil." The reason some who claim to be believers seem to have no conscience against living a lifestyle that is clearly contrary to the teachings of scripture is probably because they do not have a strong sense of the fear of the Lord.

What is the fear of the Lord? To fear the Lord means to be in awe and reverence to Him. A healthy understanding of the fear of the Lord is simply to be awestruck by His power and presence. Our Father in heaven loves us perfectly. He wants the best for our lives, but remember, He is God and we are not. He created the entire universe and has all power and authority in His hand. So as Christians, how can we not possess a holy fear of the Lord?

This is not to say that God wants us to cower in a corner, which is unhealthy fear. The Lord does not desire for His children to be afraid of Him, but to honor and respect Him. God's Word tells us that "perfect love casts out fear" (1 John 4:18). In other words, where there is God's perfect love, unhealthy fear cannot dwell. To say it another way—where there is the presence of unhealthy fear, there is the absence of love.

> Our fear of the Lord is not a destructive fear, but one that leads us to God's presence and purity.

However, if we love, honor and respect our God, we will want to obey Him, because the healthy fear of the Lord will give us a holy fear of sinning against Him and facing the consequences. Francis Chan in his book *Crazy Love* calls this having a "reverent intimacy." The fear of the Lord takes us to a place of intimacy with Him (Psalm 25:14).

I (Larry) grew up with an earthly father who loved me. I was not afraid of him. He was my father and my friend. However, whenever I was disobedient, I feared the consequences of the discipline I knew would follow. Yet, I knew that even the discipline was from a father who loved me. Our heavenly Father loves us so much, yet He hates sin, knowing it will destroy us.

When we read accounts of spiritual revivals throughout history, the fear of the Lord is mentioned again and again. God's conviction caused people to hate their sin and love Jesus with a passion. When we have a healthy sense of the fear of the Lord in our lives, we will not want to sin. "To fear the Lord is to hate evil" (Proverbs 8:13). A proper understanding of the fear of the Lord causes us to hate evil, knowing that evil displeases the Lord and destroys God's people. In other words, sincere Christians will not live a life of sin. Sin will break our communication with the God we serve, and we will not hear clearly.

The good news is this: When we repent and turn from our sin, Jesus washes us clean. And the "fear of the Lord" keeps us from going back to our old way of living. The Bible tells us in Acts 9:31 that the believers were "walking in the fear of the Lord." In Revelation 1:17, John had an encounter with God. "When I saw him, I fell at his feet as though dead. Then he placed his right hand on me and said: 'Do not be afraid. I am the First and the Last.'"

Living in the fear of the Lord will cause us to hear His voice. Our fear of the Lord is not a destructive fear, but one that leads us to God's presence and purity. When we under-

**REFLECTION**

*Define the fear of the Lord in your own words.*

stand and experience the fear of the Lord, we will hate sin and turn away from it. We will trust Jesus to wash, cleanse and make us new.

Our God is a God of complete authority in the universe. Let's ask the Lord to give us the grace today to understand what it looks like to be awestruck by Him. Within your moments of silence, expect to experience the fear of the Lord!

## Rest and Retreat Can Break the Silence

**DAY 4**

Our friend Merle Shenk, who lives with his family in Cape Town, South Africa, grew up in a society that prided itself on working hard and accomplishing much. He learned early in life that achievements equaled being successful. Being taught workaholic tendencies from a young age made it easy for him to transfer the same mentality into his spiritual walk with God.

"I began to think that God was pleased with me because of my achievements. I saw God more as a benevolent taskmaster than a Father with unconditional love. I was predisposed to believe that the more I achieved, the more God would love me and that I somehow needed to earn God's love by doing a little bit extra. I thought that God wanted me to run in "ultra-productive mode.""

Eventually, no matter how much Merle prayed and strived, God didn't seem to be talking. Merle tried to "do" more in order to "get" His attention, but it didn't work. It seemed that no matter what Merle did, he could not make God speak to him.

Merle said, "I was used to getting results when I wanted them. I was used to being able to rethink problems and find solutions. My culture told me to bear down and push harder."

Eventually Merle ran out of emotional gas. At the prompting of his wife and one of his spiritual mentors, he went away to the mountains to be completely alone. Merle says, "My wife told me, 'I don't care if you don't come back with fresh vision, I don't care if you don't come back with anything, just rest.' I did. I was determined to rest as long as it took. I slept, I sat in the woods, I listened to the wind blowing through the trees, and I removed every agenda from my heart except to rest."

Heading into this time away, he thought that he would go mad. "What was I going to do without an agenda and something to accomplish"? Despite his misgivings, he settled on the agenda of rest. It was the only thing that he allowed himself to do. After five days of almost complete silence, God began to speak to Merle's heart.

> I was predisposed to believe that the more I achieved, the more God would love me and that I somehow needed to earn God's love by doing a little bit extra.

"The silence was broken. God showed me how I had succumbed to busyness and work. He spoke to me about how I was actually wanting God to enforce my will with His power, instead of getting close to Him to hear His agenda. My identity was not to be found in my accomplishments but found in Him. His love for me was not tied to my accomplishments, like it was in the eyes of man."

Now, when he notices that he is depending on what he is doing for God rather than finding his identity in God, Merle knows that he needs to pull back and take time to rest. God says that the Sabbath is for man. He gives us rest and wants us to work with Him from that place. We have heard it said and found it to be true, "The rest place is the best place."

The Bible says, "For thus says the Lord God, the Holy One of Israel: 'In returning and rest you shall be saved; In quietness and confidence shall be your strength" (Isaiah 30:15). Sometimes we need to go to a place of solitude in order to hear from the Lord. The turmoil around us and the clamoring of everyday living, can block out our ability to hear God speaking.

**REFLECTION**

*Are you in the midst of chaos or a chaotic situation or lifestyle?*

Sharon Daugherty, author and teacher at Victory Christian Center in Tulsa, Oklahoma, writes of a time she struggled with maintaining God's peace. In her book, *Walking in the Spirit*, she writes of sensing God speaking to her heart, "Come apart, Sharon, before you come apart."[1]

Let us take to the hills of retreat and solitude to meet with God and listen for His voice amidst the quiet and rest. Expect to hear his voice speaking to your spirit.

# Start Moving

Merle Shenk told us the humorous story of a man who brought his wife to a marriage counselor. After sitting down and discussing the friction and pain that was happening in their marriage, the marriage counselor got up from behind the desk, walked over to the man's wife and gave her a big, long hug. As the wife began to sob from this simple act of kindness, the frustration and pain that had been pent up for weeks was visibly relieved. The counselor turned to the husband and with a tone of instruction said, "Do you see that this is all your wife really needs?" The husband replied with enthusiasm, "Yes, I see! I will bring her back here for a hug every Tuesday and Friday."

Merle went on to say, "At times I have recognized in myself the desire for God to take back responsibility for the very thing that He is asking for me to take responsibility. I want Him to create a loving environment in my home for my children. I want Him to give me financial soundness and stability. I want my wife to feel loved! In short, I want to defer my God given responsibility back to God. I have a desire in my human nature to escape the process, but the learning curves that He has laid out in my life will ultimately cultivate my relationship with Him and others. When I bypass the process, I miss out on a deeper appreciation for life and the opportunity to add value to my involvement with others. I have found that most of the time, God does not answer the prayers where I ask Him to detour from the process. At least not in the way that I want Him to do so!"

When the motivations of our prayers are based on fear and disobedience to the instruction that God has given, our perspective becomes cloudy. In this place, we lose sight of the vision that God has given to us. When we embrace God-given responsibility and commit to walking through with the assigned task that He has given, God helps us. As we step out in faith to face these challenges, our perspective changes. Suddenly we are no longer asking God to remove us from our obligations but to guide us through them. As we do this, our own perspective changes and we begin to see God's hand ordering and directing our steps again.

> "Many people are waiting on God, but God is waiting on us."

The following two scriptures seem contradictory but are not in actuality. "So Jesus answered and said to them, 'Have faith in God'" (Matthew 11:22 NKJV). "Then the Apostles told the Lord, 'Give us more faith!'" (Luke 17:5 ISV).

In one scripture Jesus is saying, "Have faith in God" and in the other scripture, the disciples are saying, "Increase our faith." This is the classic scenario in our lives when we want God to do what He has instructed us to do. One preacher said it this way: "Many people are waiting on God, but God is waiting on us."

Many times we have prayed for the lost to be saved. We plea, "Lord, bring your salvation to my city, to my neighborhood, to my street," but often it is not until we fulfill His Great Commission to "go," that His salvation will come to our city. Sometimes when God seems to be silent, He is simply waiting for us to obey the scriptures that He has already spoken in His Word.

**REFLECTION**
*What are some examples where your life was enriched by embracing your God-given responsibility? What did you learn through this process?*

Another important truth we want to share with you: Never move too quickly on important decisions. The Bible tells us, "It is dangerous and sinful to rush into the unknown" (Proverbs 19:2 TLB). It is amazing how often we can change our minds if we just wait for a few hours or days. God is faithful. He will make the way forward clear to us.

# What We Cannot See

Often God's silence wages a great spiritual battle in our mind. His silence simply does not make sense to us. Why doesn't God answer our prayers as he promised?

Merle told us that he has heard a well-known preacher say, "You cannot have great victories without going through great battles." This is often true.

Do you remember the story of Martha and Mary when their brother Lazarus died? The Bible says, "Now Martha said to Jesus, 'Lord, if you had been here, my brother would not have died'" (John 11:21).

We don't really know what Martha was going through in the three days after her brother Lazarus died. We only know that she had sent for Jesus, but He had not come when she thought that she needed Him. There was silence. Yet God was planning a glorious event that she could not see or imagine.

It appears as if Martha was going through a great battle inside. She was struggling with grief, pain and the same hard questions that each of us experience when we walk through personal loss or tragedy. Finally, after four days of mourning, Jesus shows up. Perhaps she was secretly resentful. Here was the One who had healed so many others, the One who walked in supernatural experiences and the power of God, but He was too late when His own friend needed him.

> Remember, you cannot have a resurrection without first experiencing a death.

I (Larry) know of a young missionary whose car broke down four times in one week. The fourth time, he was left stranded along the side of the road. At that time, his finances were so tight that he found it hard to provide for his family, let alone have money to fix a car! He slumped on the ground beside his car. As tears streamed down his face, he cried out to God. The missionary questioned whether or not God had even called him to missions and ministry and doubted if anything he was giving his life for would be successful. In truth his situation was much more complicated than a broken down car, which was the final straw that led to a breaking point in his life. He was in a battle. He asked, "Where is God in all of this?"

In the next few days, someone heard about his plight. Without the missionary's knowledge, they took it upon themselves to organize money to buy his family a brand new vehicle! In a moment of great despair, when life seemed to be piling up, God was working behind the scenes to do a great miracle for him.

As Lazarus was taking his last breaths, I am sure Martha was also asking, "Where is God in all of this? Where is my friend, Jesus?"

Little did Martha know, God was preparing a far greater miracle than healing. He was preparing a resurrection. Only in death can we have resurrection. It is in the context of this very difficult circumstance in her life that Jesus declared to the world, "I am the resurrection and

**REFLECTION**

*Give an example of a spiritual battle with which you have struggled.*

the Life. He who believes in me, though He die, he shall live." Jesus supported this claim by raising a man from the dead! It was during her great struggle that God was preparing

His greatest revelation of all time. Remember, you cannot have a resurrection without first experiencing a death.

## Our Friend and Guide

Sometimes when God is silent, He is calling us into a deeper level of friendship with Him. Being a friend requires an intimate knowledge of one another. Jesus said, "I have called you friends, for everything that I heard from my Father, I have made known to you" (John 15:15).

If two people are best friends, it is rare for days to pass without one friend wanting to talk with the other. Their intimate relationship grows because they spend time sharing their hearts and being honest with one another. To grow close to God, you need to talk together daily! God wants to get to know you and speak to you "face to face," just as He did with Moses. "So the Lord spoke to Moses face to face, as a man speaks to his friend" (Exodus 33:11).

Friendship requires love. God loves you! This is why He gave the sacrifice of His Son: "All this is done by God, who through Christ changed us from enemies into his friends" (2 Corinthians 5:18).

All three persons of the Trinity—God the Father, Son and Holy Spirit—desire friendship and relationship with you. They are committed to helping you hear the voice of the Lord clearly. Just before Jesus left this earth, He promised His disciples that He would send the Holy Spirit to compensate for the loss of His personal, physical presence in their lives. John 16:12-13 says, "I have much more to say to you, more than you can now bear. But when he, the Spirit of truth, comes, he will guide you into all truth. He will not speak on his own; he will speak only what he hears, and he will tell you what is yet to come."

When vacationing, some people prefer to explore whatever and whenever they want. But they may find their independent sight-seeing trips wasted because they spend a large part of the day getting lost and trying to find their way again.

We've discovered the best use of our time comes from following a guide rather than wandering aimlessly! In addition, before planning a trip, I (Larry) go to the American Automobile Association (AAA) and get expert advice and guidance on the trip.

> I believe the Holy Spirit wants to be our AAA guide to lead us into all truth.

I believe the Holy Spirit wants to be our AAA guide to lead us into all truth. But let me remind you—the Holy Spirit does a much better job than the most competent AAA guide. Sometimes we run into unexpected glitches and the AAA guide isn't there to guide us. The Holy Spirit is *always* with us. He is our guide and closest friend. He helps us discover truth and hear from God clearly during the darkest and loneliest times.

Our God knew that we would need help in understanding His plan for us, so He sent the Holy Spirit to live inside each believer through Jesus Christ. The Bible tells us that the Holy Spirit will never leave us nor forsake us. He is our Guide, our Teacher of Truth, our Counselor, our Helper and our Comforter.

## REFLECTION
*What does it mean to you to be a friend of God?*

What an amazing friend to have by our side during every season of our lives!

# CHAPTER 4

# Walking
# in Faith

## KEY MEMORY VERSE

Therefore, there is now no condemnation
for those who are in Christ Jesus.

Romans 8:1

# The Power of Our Words

During times when God seems to be silent, we must guard the words we say to ourselves and to others. The older we get, the more we realize the power of our words. The Word of God mentions countless times about the need to be careful of our words. Matthew 12:34 says, "For out of the abundance of the heart the mouth speaks." In other words, we believe with our heart but what we speak is often what we really believe. Life and death are in the power of the tongue (Proverbs 18:21).

By our speech, we can pronounce either a blessing or a curse on ourselves and others. If we continually say, "I think I'm going to get sick," we begin to pronounce a curse of sickness on our lives. Instead we should say, "I feel like I'm getting sick, but I know that God desires for me to be whole, and I receive His healing in Jesus' name." By speaking words of faith, we pronounce a blessing over our lives.

Sometimes people say, "Since my mother or father suffered from depression, maybe I'll be depressed." By speaking and believing these words, we open the door for the devil to do those negative things. The enemy will attempt to use these words to plant fear, and the things that we fear can come upon us. Job 3:25 tells us, "For the thing I greatly feared has come upon me, and what I dreaded has happened to me."

Fear is destroyed as we speak the Word of God to ourselves and to others around us. According to 1 John 4:18,

"Perfect love drives out fear." God also tells us in 2 Timothy 1:7, "For God has not given us a spirit of fear, but of power and of love and of a sound mind." Your Heavenly Father was never depressed, and you are His child! "Whom the Son sets free is free!" (John 8:36). Speak the truth of God's Word to yourself. Talking to yourself is very healthy as long as you are speaking the truth of God's Word.

Earlier today I (Larry) felt tired and downcast and I began to tell myself, "I can do all things through Christ" (Philippians 4:13). Within minutes I felt completely different. But let me add words of caution: Our feelings do not always change immediately, but we continue to speak in faith.

> Let me add a word of caution: Our feelings do not always change immediately, but we continue to speak in faith.

If we say to ourselves we will never hear from God clearly, this hinders us from hearing because it allows unbelief to invade our thoughts. The Scriptures teach us that His sheep hear his voice (John chapter 10) so we know it is his will for us to hear Him speak to us. Agreeing with what God says in His Word brings faith into our lives to hear clearly (Romans 10:17).

We recently heard of a young man who struggled constantly with hearing the words playing within his mind: "You will always be alone." He felt alone in a crowded room or surrounded by his family, because he was constantly listening to that resounding voice. But God's voice (His Word) says, "He will never leave or forsake us," and "he places the lonely in families" (Hebrews 13:5 and Psalm 68:6). With every whispered lie of the devil, the Word of God will always supercede it. Applying the Word of God will help to break the silence for His Word is powerful in the midst of dark times and crisis.

**REFLECTION**
*Why are words important?*

The devil will try to use our words against us. We need to be careful how we speak. This week, let's speak the things that God says in His Word: life-giving words that release hope in our lives and in the lives of those around us.

## DAY 2

## Become a Berean

When God seems to be silent, we must focus on the truth of the Holy Scriptures, not on man's ideas.

When Paul taught from the Scriptures and gave the message of Christ in the city of Berea, the Bible says the Bereans "received the message with eagerness and examined the Scriptures every day to see if what Paul said was true" (Acts 17:11). What does this show us? Do not merely take what your favorite preacher or speaker says at face value. Make sure it lines up with the Scriptures.

I (Larry) learned many years ago that man is fallible, but God's Word never fails. There were well-known preachers to whom I looked up when I was a young man, but later they began to teach heresy that did not agree with the Word of God. As I mentioned earlier, the most important way to hear God speak is through His written Word, the Bible. This is the purest and surest way that God speaks to us. Jesus said, "If you continue in My Word, then you are truly disciples of Mine; and you will know the truth, and the truth will make you free" (John 8:31, 32). We will never go off track if we obey the Word of God. It is the clearest way He speaks to us.

The Bible is an amazing book—the most influential book in all history—the world's all-time best seller. It is the written, divine expression and revelation of God to humanity. We should read it with the expectation that God will speak to us through its words. If we listen, even during times when we feel God is silent, we can hear God's voice addressing us through its pages. Jesus set this example for us.

> The most important way of hearing God speak is through His written Word, the Bible.

Leonard Sweet said, "Nobody soaked their soul so fully in scripture as did Jesus. Every action in his life, every sermon he preached, every one of his person-to-person interactions, brought the presence of God as revealed in Scripture to light and life. Jesus constantly spoke Scripture without quoting Scripture. When he spoke Scripture, he didn't chapter and verse it. He God-breathed it. He brought together a little Isaiah, mixed with a little Hosea, to which he added a bit of Jeremiah. Jesus did not recite scripture so much as Jesus made the truth of God's Word into the truth of his life."

We are reminded of a story from our friend, Reyna Britton, who works in the medical field. She recalled struggling through a season of intense anxiety. God did not change her circumstances or take away her anxious fears. Instead she discovered a prescription—a scripture—that staved off troubling mind traffic. This verse was Isaiah 26:3 (NLT), "You will keep in perfect peace all who trust in you, all whose thoughts are fixed on you!"

Reyna explained, "I focused on the words *perfect peace.* I savored the truth that God's peace is perfect, not temporal or fleeting. I recalled often Jesus' declaration to His disciples, 'I am leaving you with a gift—peace of mind and heart. And the peace I give is a gift the world cannot give. So don't be troubled or afraid' (John 14:27). What a joy to know that I did not need to be troubled or anxious. I love how God's Word is alive and spiritually discerned."

**REFLECTION**
*How can we become like a Berean?*

The truth of God's Word is the plumb-line by which we measure all things; it brings life when God seems to be silent. John 6:63 says, "The Spirit gives life; the flesh counts for nothing. The words I have spoken to you—they are full of the Spirit

4—6—15
STart

and life." As you walk through times of darkness, allow Him to speak to you through the truth of His written Word for His truth will set you free!

**DAY 3**

# Freedom from Condemnation

Sometimes God seems to be silent because we are experiencing condemnation. Many of us feel condemned and live in shame because of wrong decisions we have made, but it is not God who condemns us. He has come to give us freedom from shame and condemnation. The battle is within our own minds.

Many confuse conviction with condemnation, but they are actually very different. The devil condemns. God convicts. What is the difference between the two? Condemnation brings doubt, fear, unbelief, shame and hopelessness. Satan condemns to bring us down and destroy our faith. Conviction convinces us of error and compels us to admit

> Many confuse conviction with condemnation, but they are polar opposites. The devil condemns. God convicts.

the truth. God convicts us to restore us to faith and right standing with Him. Our God always corrects us to build us up, and His conviction always brings hope and a way towards freedom.

Oswald Chambers said, "Conviction of sin is one of the most uncommon things that ever happens to a person. It is the beginning of an understanding of God. Jesus Christ said that when the Holy Spirit came, He would convict people of sin. When the Holy Spirit stirs a person's conscience and brings him into the presence of God, it is not that person's relationship with others that bothers him, but his relationship with God."

Conviction moves us to look at what God offers and challenges us to know this infinite, loving and almighty heavenly Father. True conviction is entirely different from condemnation. God's voice brings conviction and offers an escape route from that sin. The enemy's voice brings condemnation with no way out.

A friend shared a time when he constantly heard a barrage of condemning thoughts whenever he attempted to pray: "You can't expect God to answer your prayers, remember what you have done." The fact was that he had indulged in pornography. Although he had repented of his sin, Satan was

**REFLECTION**
*Can you distinguish between condemnation and conviction of the Holy Spirit?*

eager to accuse and keep him in bondage by using shame and guilt. My friend learned to combat Satan's accusations with God's promises such as, "If we confess our sins, he is faithful and just to forgive us our sins and cleanse us from all unrighteousness I John 1:9."

Don't accept condemnation from Satan or from other people. "Therefore, there is now no condemnation for those who are in Christ Jesus" (Romans 8:1). Replace words and thoughts of condemnation with the truth of God's Word. When we are real with God and submit completely to Jesus Christ, He sets us completely free! Thank Him for His freedom in your life, and your thoughts and emotions will begin to line up with the truth found in the Word of God. Life is too short to live in shame and condemnation. Choose freedom today.

# Responses to Personal Criticism

Sometimes improperly processing criticism can keep us from hearing the Lord speak clearly to us. Most of us hate to be criticized, but criticism is a part of life. We have found we can choose from five different responses to criticisms that we receive.

1.  **Disregard the criticism**, throw it out and never think of it again. Assume the person criticizing us has some real issues in his/her life and what he/she said is not worth listening to anyway. Mentally defend yourself and all the reasons why the critic is a mean-spirited person.

2.  **Dwell on what was said** by rehashing it over and over again. Wake up each morning remembering what was said. Enter into a deep hole of condemnation.

3. **Criticize the person who criticized us** and let them know how their words are misguided. After all, they have no business criticizing us. They have never walked in our shoes.

4. **Tell lots of people about the criticism** and make a case as to why we are right and the offender is wrong. We can give the offense we have taken to our friends, and they end up receiving a borrowed offense. They will find it difficult to be released from their ill feelings regarding the person we told them about since they borrowed the offense from us and are defiled.

Each of the above four responses is unhealthy and the enemy will use our response to try to destroy us. There is a much bigger picture and number five is the proper response to criticism.

5. **Examine and discover truth in the criticism even if it is only 1%** and use it as an impetus for change and personal growth. In this way, we can dismiss the remainder of the criticism that is not true and refuse to allow it to tear us down or condemn us. We can count on God to convict us if a criticism is valid. When I (Larry) am not sure, I share this with a few Christian friends whom I trust to speak the truth in love to me. I have found this response is the wisest as God continues to develop me into the image of Christ.

God is an amazing sculptor. He is chiseling off anything that does not look like Jesus. Sometimes it takes the chisel of criticism to deal with extra baggage in our lives that we simply do not see. We sometimes ask people for constructive criticism, knowing it will help us grow.

As we have been learning in this book, look to the Word of God to align or correct your life. It is in the Word that you will find truth for yourself and others. Romans 8:1 says, "Therefore, there is now no condemnation for those who are in Christ Jesus." If a criticism is causing you to feel condemned, do not allow its roots to take place in your heart! If a root of bitterness begins to grow, it may be time to drop to your knees and ask for the strength of the Lord's forgiveness and grace. The scriptures teach us that we need to "look carefully lest we fall short of the grace of God; lest any root of bitterness springing up cause trouble, and by this many become defiled" (Hebrews 12:15).

> God is an amazing sculptor. He is chiseling off anything that does not look like Jesus. Sometimes it takes the chisel of criticism to deal with extra baggage in our lives that we simply do not see.

Many times, it is within our darkest and most silent moment that we hear the echoing voices of negative criticism. The enemy knows when you are at your weakest and will strike accordingly. But His grace is sufficient for you and

His power is perfected in your weakness (2 Corinthians 12:9). This verse goes on to say, "Most gladly, therefore, I will boast about my weaknesses, so that the power of Christ may dwell in me. Therefore I am well content with weaknesses, with insults, with distresses, with perse-

**REFLECTION**

*What are some wrong ways to respond to criticism?*

cutions, with difficulties, for Christ's sake; for when I am weak, then I am strong." Allow the God of the universe to be your advocate. What greater representation could you have in the midst of great criticism?

# Looking Through History

**DAY 5**

God can to speak to us through history so that we can learn from the past. God is not haphazard or random. There is continuity and unity in God's plan of dealing with mankind throughout the ages. History is doomed to repeat itself if we do not learn from the past. In the New Testament, Paul warns the early Christians to not to fall into the same sin as the murmuring, rebellious Israelites in the Old Testament. He didn't want this kind of history to repeat itself.

"Now these things occurred as examples to keep us from setting our hearts on evil things as they did" (1 Corinthians 10:6).

When the Israelites complained because of the monotonous manna, they were punished because they refused to trust and obey God. History was repeating itself in the early church. The early Christians were tempted to participate in the feasts celebrated in the pagan temples, and the apostle warned them to not expose themselves to this immorality and disobey God like the Israelites did in the past. He is, in essence, encouraging them to hear God through history so they won't make the same mistakes.

If God does something in the past, he does so for a reason—to teach us a lesson for the future. For example, take the prophet Elijah. We normally think of Elijah as a super prophet who heard God and had a special direct-line communication with Him. Elijah must have been extraordinary if he got transported into heaven without dying, right? In James 5, we see that he was not superhuman, but a mere man, like you and me. He was subject to weaknesses, and he was liable to limitations as we are.

> Many times I think I am facing a difficulty that no one else has ever faced, only to find out by reading a book that people in generations before me faced the same dilemmas.

"Elijah was a man just like us. He prayed earnestly that it would not rain, and it did not rain on the land for three and a half years. Again he prayed, and the heavens gave rain, and the earth produced its crops" (James 5:17-19). God worked a miracle in answer to Elijah's prayer, and since he is "just like us," it is reasonable to presume that God will also hear our prayers in the same way he heard and blessed Elijah.

A few years ago, I (Larry) joined thousands of Korean youth in a stadium in Seoul, Korea. They were praying all night for another visitation of the Lord's Spirit like the revival that happened in the early 1900s, when a series of mighty revivals began in Wales and spread throughout central Europe, Norway, Scandinavia and even to Africa, India, China and Korea. We were praying for history to repeat itself and for God to bring another awakening to many nations.

Acts 2:17-18 declares it loud and clear: "In the last days, God says, I will pour out my Spirit on all people. Your sons and daughters will prophesy, your young men will see visions, your old men will dream dreams. Even on my servants, both men and women, I will pour out my Spirit in those days, and they will prophesy." This scripture does not say He "might" pour out His Spirit. It says He will. This scripture was fulfilled at Pentecost, yet God desires an even greater fulfillment as thousands more receive the outpouring of his Holy Spirit. He is simply asking us to pray.

**REFLECTION**

*What is the difference between the prophet Elijah and you?*

From Genesis to Revelation, God spoke. If we listen for His voice throughout biblical history, we can hear Him speak to us today. He reveals himself to us in ways we can understand, because He never changes. Many times I think I am facing a difficulty that no one else has ever faced, only to find out by reading a book that people in generations before me faced the same dilemmas. By reading their stories, I discover how they overcame their problems and the Lord uses it to speak to me to find answers to my own problems. When God seems silent, listen to the voice of God speaking through history.

## The Family of Christ

When we feel God is silent, He may be speaking through the church. God provides other believers who can also help us hear from God. Although we live in a global planet that links us with someone halfway across the world with a click of the internet connection, communication alone does not give us the authentic fellowship we need with other people. Today people are looking for genuine relationships that give them a real sense of being understood and loved. We need community. Within this busy world, where can we find this kind of *bona fide* fellowship with others? One of God's purposes for the local church is to provide a community of believers who interact to encourage each other to hear from God.

I read the story about a young man who had given his life to God, but after a time of disappointment and disillusionment, he began to withdraw from other Christians.

The young man's pastor stopped in for a visit one cold winter evening and with the wind howling outside, they sat and talked. After some time, the wise pastor walked over to the fireplace and with a pair of prongs picked up a hot coal from the fire and placed it on the bricks in front of the fireplace. He continued to converse with the young man. Then glancing at the ember on the bricks, he said, "Do you see that piece of coal? While it was in the fireplace it burned brightly, but now that it's alone, the ember has almost gone out." The pastor walked over to the fireplace, and with the prongs, picked up the ember and placed it inside the fireplace. Within minutes, the dying ember was again burning brightly.

> When we move away from the warmth and encouraging fires of fellow believers in the body of Christ, we will eventually cool down spiritually.

It dawned on the young man what the pastor was trying to tell him. When we move away from the warmth and encouraging fires of fellow believers in the body of Christ, we will eventually cool down spiritually. Joining with others as a community of believers in a local church body helps keep our fires glowing. From that day on, the young man made a decision to join regularly with other believers in a local church in his community. He did not want to take the chance of his fire going out again.

The Bible says, "But encourage one another daily, as long as it is called today, so that none of you may be hardened by sin's deceitfulness" (Hebrews 3:13). It is extremely difficult to live the Christian life alone. Believers need to fellowship together and encourage one another daily.

The church of Jesus Christ is people, not a building or meeting. As believers, we are the church. The word church literally means called out ones. We are a group of people who have been called out of spiritual darkness into the light of God's kingdom. Every believer needs a "support system" to survive. We get that support system from being committed to other believers in a local church and having regular fellowship with them.

Although the church is not perfect, God designed the church to be a blessing to believers. Today's church has spots and wrinkles, but she is still engaged to the bridegroom and He is committed to make her beautiful. We are a part of a spiritual family. This spiritual family gives us a place to grow and learn from other believers on how to live our Christian lives. We need input from other believers in Christ, especially during seasons of feeling God's silence. Serving in our local church family also gives us the opportunity to be a blessing to others.

**REFLECTION**

*Why is a community of believers so important to hearing from God?.*

## The Local Church and Spiritual Leaders

I have had the privilege of traveling to six continents of the world. Everywhere I go, I find believers from completely different backgrounds, skin colors and cultures who have one thing in common. They all have received Jesus Christ as Lord and are part of the same family—the church of Jesus Christ.

But the word church also refers to the local body of Christ. Within God's universal church family are local churches, which provide the support and love that each believer needs. Whether you are a part of a local community church, a large mega church, or a small house church, the Lord wants to speak to you through the leadership and through fellow believers. Our God speaks to us through His family.

> When we fellowship with other believers, we realize that we are not alone in the temptations that we face.

Sometimes, through disillusionment, disappointment or spiritual pride, believers find themselves uninvolved in a local church. This leaves them very vulnerable. The local church is often the relief and support that the Lord has prepared for His people during an onslaught of the devil. When we continue in fellowship with other believers, we realize that we are not alone in the temptations that we face. We receive spiritual protection, strength, account-ability and oversight from the spiritual leaders the Lord has placed in our lives. The Lord's plan is to use the local church to protect us, help us grow and equip us to be all that we can be in Jesus Christ.

Spiritual leaders as well as other believers in the local church are there to exhort you, comfort you and uphold you in prayer. God places spiritual leaders in our lives who are accountable to God and others in order to watch out for us. "Remember your leaders, who spoke the Word of God to you. Consider the outcome of their way of life and imitate their faith. Obey your leaders and submit to their authority. They keep watch over you as men who must give an account. Obey them so that their work will be a joy, not a burden, for that would be of no advantage to you" (Hebrews 13:7, 17).

**REFLECTION**

*Why is a community of believers important to hearing from God?*

Spiritual leaders in our lives give us spiritual protection and God often uses them as His mouthpiece to speak to us. The Bible tells us that the devil is like a roaring lion seeking to devour us (1 Peter 5:8). Lions prey on strays, those who are isolated from the herd. That's why we need church leaders—to protect and encourage us. It is clearly written in 1 Thessalonians 5:12-13, "Now we ask you, brothers, to respect those who work hard among you, who are over you in the Lord and who admonish you. Hold them in the highest regard in love because of their work. Live in peace with each other."

I have been blessed again and again by the spiritual leaders that the Lord has placed in my life. Our small group leaders, local pastors and elders have provided me with a tremendous sense of encouragement and protection. Many times, these precious brothers and sisters in Christ have prayed, encouraged and exhorted us in our greatest hour of need.

God will be faithful to speak to you through spiritual leaders and fellow believers. Although God may seem to be silent, He may be trying to speak wisdom, truth and comfort to you through the family of Christ and the spiritual leadership He has placed in your life.

*End 4-6-15*

# CHAPTER 5

# Recognizing His Voice

## DAY 1

# A Still, Small Voice

When God seems to be quiet, He often speaks to us through a "still, small voice." This comes from the story of God speaking to Elijah in the quiet of his heart. Elijah discovered that when God was not heard in the mighty wind, earthquake and fire, he heard Him speak with the sound of a gentle whisper known to his heart (1 Kings 19:12).

The quiet whisper captured Elijah's attention, because it was a tender communication from a loving Father who came to encourage Elijah in a personal way. This steady, inner voice gave him specific guidance in a time of need.

God often speaks quietly to our spirits, nudging us to obey His voice. We are reminded of a story that our daughter told us while spending a week in England. She had been going through a long season of feeling as if the Lord was not speaking to her in the midst of her struggles. She awoke one morning and decided to go for a run on the busy streets of London. As she swerved in and out among the crowds of walkers, she heard a still, small voice saying, "Stop."

> As she swerved in and out among the crowds of walkers, she heard a still, small voice saying, "Stop."

She recalls thinking it was her own thoughts, but she kept hearing the simple word roll around in her mind, until she physically stopped and asked, "Is that you, God?" She immediately felt His presence and the stirring of His voice in her heart. He replied, "Yes. Stop running and just be with me." This seemingly ordinary moment was one that changed her life and impacted her steps toward intimacy with the Lord like she had never experienced before.

Many times, we are looking for the Lord to speak to us in an earth-shattering way, but He usually speaks to us by Holy Spirit-inspired impressions, thoughts and feelings. We really should pay attention to those impressions that come to us. For example, have you ever been driving down the road and had a spur-of-the-moment thought that you should pray for someone? Most would agree that this is God speaking to us in His still, small voice and that we should pray for that person.

**REFLECTION**

*Has God ever prompted you to do something by an inner nudge that you recognized as His still, small voice in your spirit? Describe what happened.*

We like the way Mark Virkler describes this "God voice" in our hearts, "God's inner voice comes to us as spontaneous thoughts, visions, feelings or impressions. Therefore, when I tune to God, I tune to chance-encounter thoughts or spontaneous thoughts."[1]

Many of the major decisions in our lives have come as a result of that quiet voice and because of the gentle nudge of the Lord over a period of time. Sensitivity to the Holy Spirit causes us to hear when He speaks. The Lord desires to speak to us by this witness of the Spirit. The Bible says,

"The Spirit himself testifies with our spirit that we are God's children" (Romans 8:16).

The mind receives head knowledge, but the spirit receives a deeper sense of knowing by the Holy Spirit. Many times when we are teaching, the Lord drops a new thought into our spirit that we share although it was not in our notes. This is God speaking through the Holy Spirit who causes us to be sensitive to Him. Let's learn to listen for the still small voice of the Lord within us. It may be just the word we need to break the silence!

## Recognizing that Inner Voice

**DAY 2**

Let's dig a little deeper into the quiet whispers of the Lord. Many times we hear a voice within us, but excuse it as "just us." It may be God! Take that inner voice seriously.

These divine or heavenly nudges are God's way of sending messages to us. God gives these impulses to guide and encourage us in our walk with Him. They may be what some pass off as just coincidental, but in time God will confirm that these inner special nudges of conviction are from Him.

Remember, your spirit and soul dwell inside of your body. It is only your spirit that will live forever. We are learning how to communicate with the Holy Spirit. The Lord wants to teach us to trust the Holy Spirit to speak to our spirits.

The Bible says, "The lamp of the Lord searches the spirit of a man; it searches out his inmost being" (Proverbs 20:27). Your spirit is a light the Lord has illuminated. He will throw its rays into the darkest recesses of the heart, so you will know how to distinguish right from wrong. You can trust this "Holy Ghost flashlight" to hear God's still, small voice speak.

One of our friends told us that he hears the Lord speak most often while mowing the lawn and taking a shower than at any other times. Why? We often hear God when we are doing some activity that has become automatic for us (exercising, cooking, cleaning) because our minds are free to receive through our spirits.

We often believe that hearing God's voice is complicated, but it is really not as hard as we may think. When we were preparing to become missionaries as a young couple, we had two choices. Our mission board told us there were openings in the states of Connecticut and South Carolina. But God seemed to be silent. We had no preference. Eventually, as

> We didn't hear God speak in an audible voice, but the feeling kept getting stronger.

we prayed, the Lord placed a burden on our hearts for the people on an island off the coast of South Carolina. We didn't hear God speak in an audible voice, but the inner nudge kept getting stronger. We knew it was the right place.

We had this sense or "nudge" in our spirit that it was right. God confirmed this intuitive conviction, and we served on John's Island, South Carolina, during the following year.

When we are really serious about listening to Him, we can expect an answer from the Lord. The scriptures tell us, "In his heart a man plans his course, but the Lord determines his steps" (Proverbs 16:9).

Look back over your life and see how the Lord has directed your steps. Sometimes God speaks by placing a desire or burden in our hearts that we know would not be from anyone else but God. We just have a certain intuitive conviction that gives us faith.

Rest assured that you will learn to recognize that inner voice from the Lord that you come to know as God's voice. His voice is one of love and concern

**REFLECTION**

*How does sensitivity to the inner witness of the Holy Spirit help you to hear from God?*

for your well-being. Listen for and learn the ways in which He speaks to you. In time, you will begin to know and understand His voice in ways you have not experienced in the past. The silence will be broken.

## What Energizes You?

Sometimes, when God seems to be silent, the Lord is nudging us to recognize how He has created us. He desires us to follow His divine motivation in our lives to fulfill His purposes. From conception, we have each been given different motivational gifts that energize us. God speaks to us through these gifts. Maybe He is not silent after all. He may be speaking through the way that He created us!

As Romans 12:4-6 says, "Just as each of us has one body with many members, and these members do not all have the same function, so in Christ we who are many form one body, and each member belongs to all the others. We have different gifts, according to the grace given us."

If you have a motivational gift of giving, the Lord will probably speak more often to you about giving than to the average person. This is because you were made to love to give. God wants you

> Do not spend your life trying to do what you are not gifted to do.

to enjoy what you are doing. If you cannot sing in tune, the Lord is not calling you to be a worship leader. That would waste your time as well as God's true call on your life because He has not created you for musical endeavors. Some people think that if the Lord asks them to do something, it will be something that they hate doing. This could not be farther from the truth! God created you perfectly to fulfill His purposes through you.

You should ask yourself, "What burns in the depths of my spirit? What desire is in there? Am I hungry to learn more, to serve the kingdom, to be a business owner, to be a pastor, a missionary, a prophet, an intercessor, an entrepreneur or be used in the ministry of helping others?" A great evidence that these thoughts are not mere daydreams of your mind is to ask, "Is my heart overflowing with joy and faith when I think about these things?" There is a purpose of God to be fulfilled in your life. God often answers these questions through our natural gifts, abilities and unique talents He bestowed upon us.

If you aren't sure of your purpose in life, do what you are good at doing and watch God confirm you by blessing your endeavors. Do not spend your life trying to do what you are not gifted to do. I (Larry) tried to minister to children in a Sunday school class, but soon realized it was not my gift. When we started our new church, I preached one Sunday and ministered to the children in Sunday school the next. Those poor kids put up with me every other week! Teaching in the children's ministry was not my gift.

Genesis 4:20-22 tells us that Jabal was the father of those who raised cattle. His brother Jubal was the father of all the musicians who played the lyre and pipe. His half-brother

**REFLECTION**
*How do you generally hear God speaking?*

Tuabal-Cain forged instruments made of bronze and iron. They were all different with specific gifts from the Lord.

God has made you uniquely and you are one of a kind. He will speak to you and lead you according to the way He has shaped you for His service. Many times, when we have asked God what He wanted us to do in a specific situation, He has spoken to our hearts, "Do what you want to do." God gives us more and more liberty as we grow spiritually into a state of maturity just like we do with our own children. When they were young and inexperienced, we made all of their decisions for them; but as they grew older and mature, we let them make choices according to their preferences.

Maybe you are trying to hear from God concerning choices in your life. In actuality, He is speaking to you through the way He has made you. Trust those inner leadings and nudges that come from the way God wired you.

*Stoped 5-6-15*

## What Next?

**DAY 4**

Our God not only wants us to listen so He can tell us what to do, but He also wants us to listen so we know what not to do. Jesus said that He would send the Holy Spirit to indwell us and convict us of sin. When the Holy Spirit convicts us, we see how desperately we need God. God doesn't convict us of our sins to expose us and make us feel bad. Instead, He wants to make us feel desperate for Him, realizing we have no confidence in ourselves.

The Holy Spirit's conviction is intended to convince us to repent, which means to turn and go in the right direction leading us towards righteousness rather than the wrong one. In other words, if we are behaving in a way that is not pleasing to God, we must be willing to make an adjustment in our lives. If we don't, our hearts become hardened.

Hardened hearts are the result of ignoring the Holy Spirit's conviction of right and wrong. The more hard-hearted we become, the more difficult it is for us to quickly hear and promptly obey the Lord.

If I am angry at someone, bitterness can grow in my heart. However, if I allow the Holy Spirit and the Word of God to quickly prompt me to forgive, I can receive grace to move on and hear the Lord speak accurately. God loves to transform people. It is a promise in His Word. He said that He would take our hardened hearts and give us a heart that is sensitive to the touch of our God.

> This conviction might come from an inner prompting of God's still, small voice, by reading the Word of God, by hearing a sermon preached or in an unconventional way.

It is healthy and normal to feel guilty when we are initially convicted of sin; however, if we keep feeling guilty after we have repented, it is spiritually unhealthy. It is good to know that the Holy Spirit doesn't spring everything on us at once. He sometimes convicts us to change or make adjustments in our lives one step at a time. This allows us the opportunity to truly take steps toward meaningful and lasting change!

The Lord invites us to approach Him without being afraid. The Bible says He wants to help us in our time of need. "Let us then approach the throne of grace with confidence, so that we may receive mercy and find grace to help us in our time of need" (Hebrews 4:16). If we have sin in our lives, our heavenly Father still loves us. He wants us to come boldly to His throne and receive His forgiveness, grace, and mercy!

God's conviction fell on a bakery owner in Bristol, England, while George Mueller was praying for food for his orphanages. God awakened a bakery owner across town who felt God's conviction to get up, call an employee and ask him to go to the shop to bake a day's bread for the orphans. Then on second thought, he told the employee, "Bake enough for a month, so I can get some sleep."[1]

God is speaking to us when He convicts us. This conviction might come from an inner prompting of God's still, small voice, by reading the Word of God, by hearing a sermon preached or in an unconventional way. Choose today to take His conviction and move forward in His forgiveness, grace and mercy as you continue to develop a sensitivity to hear His voice and obey Him.

**REFLECTION**
*How does conviction stir your conscience to want to know God better?*

# Failure Is Not Who You Are

When we are experiencing a season of God's silence, we may be tempted to feel like a failure. Thomas Edison once said, "Anyone who has never made a mistake has never tried anything new." This is coming from the man who tried more than 1,000 times before perfecting the light bulb. He claimed he did not fail 1,000 times but rather learned to try another way to perfect the light bulb. Failure is an action or incident, but it does not define you.

A friend of ours played high school football. During one of the games, his team lost by one point. The fans blamed him for the loss and vandalized his home by scrawling nasty names on the windows of his house. The insults dug deep into his heart. When he awoke the following morning, the graffiti had been washed off the windows. His father explained, "I did not want you to see those names again. That is not who you are—you're my son and I'm proud of you."

This is how God feels about you and me! His Word says, "Do not be afraid... I have called you by name; you are mine. When you go through deep waters, I will be with you. When you go through rivers of difficulty, you will not drown. When you walk through the fire of oppression, you will not be burned up; the flames will not consume you. For I am the Lord, your God ... You are honored, and I love you. Do not be afraid, for I am with you" (Isaiah 43:1-5 NLT).

> Allow God to turn your mistakes and failures into learning experiences.

When I was a young man, God spoke through those scriptures directly into my life. They gave me the faith to go on after I felt like a failure. The keyword here is "felt." I was in God's training school, learning that failure is only an event and not who I am. It is what you do with that event that can change your course and perspective.

John Creasy, a famous novelist in England, got 753 rejection slips from publishers before he published his first book. He went on to publish 564 books. R.P. Macy failed seven times as an entrepreneur in retailing before he started Macy's department store. Can you imagine the persistence? The freedom to make mistakes is encouraged in the business world. That is why new inventions and building prototypes require a process of trial and error. From God's perspective, the same reality applies to us.

**REFLECTION**

*Have you experienced a failure that has discouraged you or caused you to quit trying?*

The Bible is filled with stories of those who failed during a season of their lives but got back up and refused to quit. From Moses to Joshua to Esther to Paul—they all made their share of mistakes, but they continued on in perseverance. They refused to quit.

Paul the apostle says, "I have fought the good fight, I have finished the race, I have kept the faith" (2 Timothy 4:7). Notice the progression in this verse. When God calls us to start, He will see us through to the finish, but there is always a fight until the end! Sometimes our greatest act of spiritual warfare is simply to not quit.

Speak truth into who you are in Christ as you dust yourself off and move forward. His Word says in Romans 8:37, "In all things we are more than conquerors through Him who loved us." What a great revelation to walk in daily!

Today is new and filled with limitless possibilities. Allow God to turn your mistakes and failures into learning experiences. Remember, if you fail or fall, you are not a failure! Get back up in Jesus' name and declare who you really are—a son and daughter of the living God! Speak His truth and walk with your head held high!

*SToped 5-18-15*

## Who Are You?

Sometimes God seems to be silent and we cannot hear clearly because we feel as if we are not righteous enough. But the truth is that Jesus has made us righteous by faith in Him. When God looks at us, He sees Jesus first! We are righteous by faith, not by what we do (Romans 5:1).

In the Chinese language, the word for "righteousness" is the combination of two pictures. On top is the figure of a lamb and directly beneath is that of a person. What a perfect image of the righteousness that Christ alone provides, namely our being covered by the Lamb of God, Jesus! Whenever the Father looks at you, He first sees the perfect Lamb of God in you. Certainly God is aware of every sin in our lives, but that isn't what He sees first and foremost. Instead, He sees the beauty of His Son enveloping us.

As we learn to walk and talk with God, we get to know His heart, His character and His ways. If we are committed to following His character and ways, He can give us a greater liberty because we become "one with Him." As our spirit becomes filled with His Spirit, and our desires begin to merge with His, we walk in His ways. Jesus said, "I and the Father are one" (John 10:30) and "I do nothing on my own but speak just what the Father has taught me" (John 5:30). Jesus was one with His Father and was given freedom by His Father on the earth. He knew His heavenly Father so well that He modeled His Father's character and only did what He saw His Father doing.

> We so often "see" with blurred vision. When we have the correct "prescription," we walk in a manner that is fitting to a child of God.

We can easily get stuck in a season of feeling like we are in the depths of despair, losing hope, and lacking direction. We cry out to God, "Where are you? I feel lost and I am not sure what do!" But most times, we are caught within this place because we do not see ourselves correctly. We are too busy seeing the things that we are not instead of the things that we are! The Bible addresses this in Romans 8:16-17, "The Spirit Himself testifies with our spirit that we are children of God, and if children, heirs also, heirs of God and fellow heirs with Christ." We are sons and daughters of the Most High God! What an identity and inheritance we have been given for free!

As we begin to see ourselves as the righteousness of Christ, the attitude we carry and the decisions we make begin to change. We are no longer cowering before the Lord and others. We hold our head high.

When we first realized that our youngest daughter, Leticia, needed glasses, she was eight or nine years old. Although she stood only a few feet from the kitchen clock, she asked for the time. We responded, "Can't you see the time? It is right in front of you!" She protested, "But, it's blurry and unclear." We immediately knew that our daughter needed glasses. When Leticia put on her new glasses, she felt like she was a part of a whole new world! Amazed, she said, "So this is what it is like to truly see!"

I imagine that this is much like our own walk with the Lord. We so often "see" with blurred vision. When we have the correct "prescription," we walk in a manner that is fitting to a child of God. In moments of seeming silence from the Lord, we can say, "I know who Jesus is; therefore, I know who I am! So I will walk in a manner befitting the royalty and righteousness of God." This is a game changer!

**REFLECTION**
*What does in mean to be righteous in Christ?*

Let's hear Him speak to us by what He reveals through His character, which extends to each of us. His unconditional love, acceptance, forgiveness and righteousness is free and alive within us. No matter where you are in your spiritual journey with Christ, God sees the beauty of Jesus in you. The key is for you to see it for yourself and to walk in a manner befitting a child of the King!

## The Unexpected Speaker

**DAY 7**

A friend of ours was facing a time in life when she felt discouraged and stretched thin. Then God unexpectedly spoke to her through an unlikely source—a Barbie story book. She had stopped at a grocery store to pick up some items so she could bake a treat for her elderly grandparents. As she stood waiting in line at the checkout, she inwardly grumbled, "Do I really need to take time for my elderly grandparents when I have so many other obligations?"

She absentmindedly picked up a children's story book and browsed through the story about how Barbie was scheduled to be in a competition but needed to help her elderly neighbor. Subsequently, she arrived late to the competition; however, the judges were so impressed with her that she won the prize anyway.

Our friend heard God speaking through this children's book. She said, "I was convicted and encouraged all at the same time to continue to serve my grandparents and trust God to help take care of everything in my life. I was reminded that with God's strength and priorities, I can be a winner, too!"

To think that God used a silly children's book to penetrate our friend's darkness seems almost ridiculous. That's the amazing characteristic about God, He uses the most ordinary things in unexpected ways to speak to us.

Sometimes He even uses people we least expect to be his mouthpiece to speak to us. Surprisingly, God can speak through unsaved people to get our attention. God spoke through a heathen king of Egypt to send a message to the godly King Josiah, telling him not to go to battle. King Josiah ignored this pagan's claim to be hearing from God; he went to war anyway and was killed. God does not limit Himself to using only Christians or spiritually perfect messengers to communicate with us. If that were the case, He wouldn't use any of us as His messengers!

> Sometimes when God seems to be silent, he uses people we would never expect to speak to us.

Probably the most likely way God will speak to you through a non-Christian is through those who hold positions of authority in your life or who are an expert in their field. For example, God can speak through your unsaved boss, parent or teacher. A Christian businessman told me that one of his most trusted advisers is another businessman who is not a believer. He has been used greatly by the Lord to advise my friend in matters of business. The words he speaks to my friend are the words of God for him.

Discernment is the key to knowing if you are hearing God's voice through a non-Christian's message. The truth is, the same goes for hearing God through a godly person. Either way, we need to trust we will recognize the source, because of the Holy Spirit living inside of us and helping us to recognize God's voice. This is how we can usually discern the advice or message as coming from God or not.

God wants us to grasp His purpose and message no matter how or through whom He gives it. The Bible encourages us to trust Him to direct us. Isaiah 30:21 says, "Your ears will hear a word behind you, 'This is the way, walk in it,' whenever you turn to the right or to the left.'"

God is faithful and will direct our path one step at a time. He will get us to the place He wants us to go if we lay aside our preconceived ideas as to how He will speak and tune our ears to hear His voice.

Oswald Chambers said, "Jesus rarely comes where we expect Him; He appears where we least expect Him.... The only way a servant can remain true to God is to be ready for the Lord's surprise visits. This readiness is expecting Jesus Christ at every turn. This sense of expectation will give our life the attitude of childlike wonder He wants it to have."

**REFLECTION**
*Did God ever give you an unexpected revelation that you knew was His voice speaking personally to you?*

Expect the unexpected. At times, God may speak in surprising, dramatic and unpredictable ways! Be ready and willing to hear from Him in a new way during your current season.

# CHAPTER 6

# Learning to Listen

## Take Time to Listen

Have you experienced being in love? You could not wait to spend time with that person. You easily sacrificed your time in order to make that happen. We do the same for close friends. We look forward to spending time with them. How much more does the Lover of our souls cherish time with us! He created us with this great desire for close and intimate relationship with others; but first and foremost, we were created to have a relationship with Him and then with one another.

Why is it so vitally important for every believer to have daily time alone with God? Although we may "pray without ceasing" and walk with the Lord minute by minute, designating a special time of day to be alone with the Lord is vital to relating heart-to-heart with God. It helps to give a divine rhythm to our routine as we place ourselves in a position to hear from God.

We are blessed with a great relationship as husband and wife, and often communicate through cell phone or in personal contact many times throughout the day. However, LaVerne still appreciates a special night when we can spend time alone with no distractions. We call it our "date night," and keep that regular appointment even though we have been married for more than four decades. Making time with God a daily priority is saying that our relationship with the Lord is important and therefore we will set apart concentrated time to build this relationship.

Yet frequently, Christians find it hard to commit to a daily time with God. We can easily fall into a rut of allowing our time to become an obligation.

Max Lucado writes that because some of us have tried and been unsuccessful, we practice a type of surrogate spirituality, where we rely on others to spend time with God and try to benefit from their experience. "Let them tell us what God is saying. After all, isn't that why we pay preachers? Isn't that why we read Christian books? These folks are good at daily devotions. I'll just learn from them. If that is your approach, if your spiritual experiences are secondhand and not firsthand, I'd like to challenge you with this thought: Do you do that with other parts of your life? I don't think so. You don't do that with vacations. You don't say, 'Vacations are such a hassle, packing bags and traveling. I'm going to send someone on vacation for me. When he returns, I'll hear all about it and be spared all the inconvenience.' Would you do that? No! You want the experience firsthand. You want the sights firsthand, and you want to rest firsthand. Certain things no one can do for you."

> The simple fact remains—if we truly want an intimate, grace-filled relationship with God, we need to spend time alone with Him on a regular basis.

The simple fact remains—if we truly want an intimate, grace-filled relationship with God, we need to spend time alone with Him on a regular basis. Listening to God is a firsthand experience. When we spend time listening for God to speak, He will! Our daily encounters with God place us in a position to seek Him on behalf of not only our own needs, but the needs of others as well. We are part of the body of Christ, and our priestly task is to pray and intercede for others. Our alone time with God gives us the opportunity to hear Him speak so that we can be encouraged and in turn encourage others.

Although some people easily spend an hour or more each day with God, others may start at five, ten or fifteen minutes and increase it over time. Allow the peace of God to rule in your heart (Colossians 3:15) concerning the time you believe God wants you to spend with Him.

**REFLECTION**
*Why is it important to take time alone with God every day?*

Do you hear Him calling out to you? "Arise, my love ... and come away..." (Song of Solomon 2:10). Seek a friendship with God today by giving Him your full attention. This time well-spent can be a wonderful way to hear from Him.

## DAY 2

# Our Time Alone with God

A story is told of a man, who in utter frustration asked his pastor why God had not been giving him answers. Unable to hear the pastor's mumbled reply, the man moved closer, asking the pastor to repeat what he had said. Still unable to hear the reply, he moved closer and closer until finally his ear almost touched the pastor. Then he heard the pastor's faintest whisper, "Sometimes God whispers so that we will move closer to Him." Job 33:14 says, "God does speak . . . though man may not perceive it."

As we mentioned before, spending time with God daily is crucial in our relationship with Him. Many of us do not take the time to listen and talk with the Lord of the universe each day. No wonder we feel like we cannot hear Him! God desires our closeness. He wants our unwavering love. Developing a love relationship with the Lord changes us from the depths of our beings. We will learn to hear His voice more clearly when we spend time in His Word and as we choose intentional communication with Him.

Pick a time of day that works for you to spend time alone with God. It works best for both of us to spend time alone with the Lord in the morning because that is when we are more alert and can give God our peak concentration. But your temperament may prefer another time of the day or night. Find the time that works best for you, readjust your priorities and schedule time to meet with God.

Two main activities of spending time with God are reading the Bible and praying. Reading the Bible opens the door to communication from God. The Bible is God speaking to humanity. The Bible reading plan that I (Larry) use takes me through the Bible at my own pace. Listening for God's voice but not reading God's Word will make us vulnerable to hearing voices that are not from the Lord. Many evil spirits are eager to whisper lies to us. Studying the written Word of God protects us from deception.

An idea can feel good to our emotions but fail to give us lasting peace when it isn't in line with God's Word.

Knowledge of the Word is of vital importance in discerning the voice of God. If we don't know the Word, we won't have anything with which to compare the ideas and arguments that war against God's perfect will for our lives. The devil can give us ideas that may make sense to us, but just because something seems logical does not necessarily mean it is from God. An idea can feel good to our emotions but fail to give us lasting peace when it isn't in line with God's Word.

Prayer is simply talking with God. As you spend time alone with a friend, you begin to understand your friend's hopes, dreams and desires. You do this by speaking and by taking time to listen to your friend. Communication is incomplete if you do all the talking. The more listening time you spend with your heavenly Father, the better you will understand His heart for you. Do not expect God to function simply as a drive-through fast food restaurant. While we may place our order (heart's desire), we must take time to hear His heart's desire on the matter. God always knows what is best and He has the timing exact.

God seeks to quiet the noise in order to make way for His voice to be heard. When is the last time you got away for an extended period of time without technology at your fingertips? When have you just sat and quieted yourself by the beach or simply closed the door and sat in silence waiting on God? Too often life is so harried that we rush up to God, say a few hurried prayers and rush away again.

To hear God's voice, find ways to be quiet and listen. The Bible says that Jesus departed to a lonely place to pray early in the morning. After a day's ministry, He again went to a mountain to pray and be alone with God. As you talk to God and quietly listen, you can draw on His presence and power to revitalize your spiritual life. You will begin to understand Him and know what He wants you to do. Develop a listening heart that is open to hear His voice.

**REFLECTION**
*Why is it important to focus on both prayer and the Word of God each day?*

# Prayer

God most often penetrates His silence by speaking to us in response to prayer. Psalm 91:15 says that when we call on Him, He will answer. Although we have been discussing how God speaks to us in answer to prayer, let's take a closer look at how it affects our everyday lives.

Cornell Haan, co-founder of the World Prayer Team, recalls a time when he was a rebellious teenager. When he arrived home after curfew, his mother was sitting in her chair and praying. "She did not scold me or punish me, but simply sat there, often with tears in her eyes, praying for me. Her reaction caused me to be very ashamed of my disobedience—more so than a sharp talking to or being grounded," said Haan. God heard and answered this mother's prayers and her son's life was changed. Haan said of his mother's example, "From her I learned to pray about problems more and to speak harshly less."[1]

Our prayers keep us on God's mind. They cause God to notice our heartfelt supplications. God spoke to Cornelius in the book of Acts in response to his sincere prayers. "Four days ago I was in my house praying at this hour, at three in the afternoon. Suddenly a man in shining clothes stood before me and said, 'Cornelius, God has heard your prayer and remembered your gifts to the poor. Send to Joppa for Simon who is called Peter.'" Cornelius, a Gentile, who was not yet a believer in Jesus Christ, had a generous heart. He prayed and God noticed and spoke to him. He sent an angel to tell Cornelius to invite a Jewish stranger to his home who would tell him about Jesus. God loves to answer us when we pray sincere prayers to Him.

Jesus tells two stories in the book of Luke that emphasize the importance of continuing a determined perseverance in prayer. In the first story in Luke 11, Jesus says, "Suppose one of you has a friend, and he goes to him at midnight and says, 'Friend, lend me three loaves of bread, because a friend of mine on a journey has come to me, and I have nothing to set before him.' Then the one inside answers, "Don't bother me. The door is already locked, and my children are with me in bed. I can't get up and give you anything." I tell you, though he will not get up and give him the bread because he is his friend, yet because of the man's boldness he will get up and give him as much as he needs."

"From her I learned to pray about problems more and to speak harshly less."

Just as this man gave in after repeated requests from his friend, so our God will respond after persistent prayer. Jesus went on to say: "Ask and it will be given to you; seek and you will find; knock and the door will be opened to you. For everyone who asks receives; he who seeks finds; and to him who knocks, the door will be opened." The Bible tells us that we do not have, because we do not ask. If we feel we seldom hear from God, perhaps we have stopped asking. He is waiting for us to make the next move. He already made His move toward us when He sent Jesus to the cross 2000 years ago.

Jesus told His disciples a second story in Luke 18. "In a certain town there was a judge who neither feared God nor cared about men. And there was a widow in that town who kept coming to him with the plea, 'Grant me justice against my adversary.' For some time he refused. But finally he said to himself, 'Even though I don't fear God or care about men, yet because this widow keeps bothering me, I will see that she gets justice, so that she won't eventually wear me out with her coming!' And the Lord said...'And will not God bring about justice for his chosen ones, who cry out to him day and night.'"

**REFLECTION**
*Why is it important to continue with perseverance in prayer?*

God loves to answer our prayers. But at times, we need to persevere and continue to ask until we receive the answer. So don't stop asking!

## Learning to Journal

Journaling is writing down what is in your heart—your thoughts, prayers, fears, disappointments, joys and miracles in your life. Did you ever experience a verse almost leaping off the pages of the Bible during a time alone with God? You may have read it one thousand times, but this time it really "grabs" you. God is speaking to you! Write it down so you do not lose it when you need it most. Proverbs says,

"Treasure my commandments within you. Write them on the tablet of your heart" (Proverbs 7:2,3).

We heard someone say that the only thing required of journaling is honesty. Journaling is like keeping a spiritual diary. Writing down your honest thoughts and God's responses to your requests, thoughts, feelings and insights provides a way of remembering God's activity in your life. A journal helps you to look back over time and see a written record of the Lord's dealings with your life. Rereading your journal can be a great tool that will encourage you when you seem to be experiencing God's silence.

When the prophet Habakkuk needed an answer from the Lord, the Lord replied by mentioning the importance of writing down what He said to him and waiting for a reply. "Write down the revelation and make it plain on tablets so that a herald may run with it. For the revelation awaits an appointed time; it speaks of the end and will not prove false. Though it linger, wait for it; it will certainly come and will not delay" (Habakkuk 2:2-4).

> Writing down your honest thoughts and God's responses to your requests, feelings and insights provides a way of remembering God's activity in your life.

Habakkuk was a prophet who was seeking to hear God speak. First he went to a quiet place where he was alone and waited for God to speak. He listens and "looks to hear what God will say" (Habakkuk 2:1). When God begins to speak, he tells Habakkuk to record the vision that he is sensing in his heart. God clearly showed His prophet how to dialogue with Him by using the combination of coming to a quiet place, listening and journaling.

Journaling is a written record of how God has been working in your life. Writing what God is speaking to you becomes a reminder of the revelation God has given you that has not yet come to pass. When the Lord speaks to me (Larry), I write it down so I do not forget it. There are things God spoke to me more than twenty years ago that are only now coming to pass. And those revelations often look much different than I had expected. If I had not written them down, I would no longer have them to help guide me into what God has for me today. It can be a way of holding yourself accountable to move on to spiritual maturity.

Writing is a method to be used to help you learn to discern God's voice better. In *Communion With God*, Mark and Patti Virkler believe one of the greatest benefits of using a journal during time spent with the Lord is that it allows you "to receive freely the spontaneous flow of ideas that come to your mind, in faith believing that they are from Jesus, without short-circuiting them by subjecting them to rational and sensory doubt."[1]

You can use a simple spiral-bound notebook, a fancier hardbound journal, a computer or even your cell phone to keep track of your impressions, inspired thoughts and scriptures as you write down what God is speaking to you.

Any of these methods of keeping track of hearing from God are valuable ones.

Cultivating an ever-deepening relationship with the Lord through journaling helps you to clearly think through what you believe the Lord is speaking to you. You can test it with the scriptures and read it from time to time to see how the Lord has renewed your mind, heart and spirit. You will discover that you have learned how to converse with God as you focus the eyes of your heart on God and receive fresh words from Him each day.

**REFLECTION**

*Describe what journaling is in your own words. Do you record God's activity through journaling?*

# Fasting

**DAY 5**

Prayer and fasting go hand in hand. Fasting is a discipline of intercession that carries the potential for answered prayer. When we fast and intercede, we pray and expect God to answer. Although I (Larry) have fasted many times, I still often find fasting to be quite difficult, but I have incorporated this regular spiritual discipline into my life. One of the members of our leadership team has fasted ten different times on solely liquids for forty days! That is amazing to me.

What is fasting exactly? When we fast, we are abstaining from daily nourishment for a period of time. We "starve" our bodies in order to feed our spirits. The essence of a fast is self-denial in order to turn our thoughts to God. We can hear God's voice more clearly when we fast because we find in Him sustenance beyond food. When prayer and fasting are combined, powerful things happen.

> Fasting is a discipline of intercession that carries the potential for answered prayer.

In Mark 9, Jesus healed a boy with an evil spirit. The disciples asked Jesus afterwards, "Why could we not cast him [the evil spirit] out"? Jesus replied, "This kind can come out only by prayer and fasting." Jesus was challenging them to maintain a life of prayer and fasting so that their faith remained firm.

Maintaining a life of prayer and fasting is paramount to hearing from God. Fasting is not an option for Christians who are serious about their walk with God. One time as Jesus was teaching on prayer and fasting, He used the term "When you fast," and went on and made His point (Matthew 6:16). Notice, he did not say, "If you fast. . . ." Jesus knew that fasting would open up a whole new realm of revelation for Christians and make it easier for them to hear the voice of the Holy Spirit.

In addition to increasing our capacity to receive from the Lord, fasting has a way of quieting all the background noise of life so we can tune in to His voice.

I love the Bible story about Daniel. In Daniel chapter 10, we read that Daniel had fasted for a period of three weeks when an angel appeared to him and said, "Since the first day that you set your mind to gain understanding . . . I have come in response . . . I have come to explain to you what will happen. . . ." Daniel had a question that he was asking the Lord, and the answer came to him as he was fasting.

God showed Moses the pattern for the tabernacle on the mountain during fasting. Queen Esther instructed her Jewish brethren to fast for three days and three nights before she appeared before the king in order to plead for the lives of her people. God answered by giving her favor with the king. The Bible is filled with examples of godly men and women receiving direction from the Lord as a result of fasting.

Although I believe we are all called to fast at certain times, we must avoid legalistic approaches to fasting. God gives grace for some individuals to fast for longer or shorter periods of time. If you have never fasted before, ask God for His grace to experience the blessing of fasting.

What if you fast and the Lord does not speak to you in a significant way? This really is the wrong question to ask. What if you fast and He does speak to you? We know it is His will for

**REFLECTION**
*How do prayer and fasting go hand-in-hand?*

us to fast, so we can trust that He will honor our obedience as we seek His voice through prayer and fasting. "But when you fast, put oil on your head and wash your face, so that it will not be obvious to men that you are fasting, but only to your Father, who is unseen; and your Father, who sees what is done in secret, will reward you" (Matthew 6:17-18).

Take the time to practice fasting in your life. Watch and see how this discipline will please your heavenly Father and bring clarity to your life. *stopped 6-15-15*

## Knowing His Character

**DAY 6**

After more than forty years of a loving marriage, LaVerne and I know each other's character. We are both confident that we would not intentionally speak harmful words or make rash decisions that would hurt or betray one another. All of our actions, including words of correction, are for our own good because we love each other. We have learned to trust each other's character.

How we see the character of God affects our relationship with Him. Since God will never tell us to do anything that is outside His character, we must get to know the very nature of God so we can hear from Him. We must understand His compassionate nature and how He longs for our intimacy and trust.

One of the most familiar verses in the Bible is John 3:16, "For God so loved the world. . . ." God's nature is revealed in this revelation of God as the Lover of mankind. We are precious in His sight and He yearns for us. He wants to reveal Himself to us and He is passionately pursuing us!

The familiar scripture verse goes on to say that God so loved the world that "He gave. . . ." He not only wants us to be lovers of people, but He also wants us to be givers. He wants us to act like He does—to live by His character. For example, He always tells the truth. He sets the example for us to do the same and to be true to our word.

The Bible tells us in Psalm 103:7 that God "made known His ways to Moses, his deeds to the children of Israel." Because Moses was in relationship with the Lord, he became acquainted with the ways of God. Moses had learned to know the character of God; however, the children of Israel only saw the things that God did because they did not have a personal relationship with Him. When we get to know God and develop a love relationship with Him, we will know what God wants us to do. He will "make known" His ways to us. Understanding this truth can break the silence we may be feeling.

> By learning the character of God, we are able to know and "hear" the way in which we should go.

1 Corinthians 13:4-8 offers us a description of love. When we substitute "God" for "love" in these verses, we get an accurate picture of God's character. "God is patient, God is kind, God does not envy, God does not boast, God is not proud, God is not rude, God is not self-seeking, God is not easily angered, God keeps no record of wrongs, God does not delight in

evil but rejoices with the truth, God always protects, God always trusts, God always hopes, God always perseveres, God never fails."

God's love is revealed so that mankind can be liberated. The Scriptures tell us the Lord is one "who forgives all your iniquities, who heals all your diseases, who redeems your life from destruction, who crowns you with loving kindness and tender mercies," (Psalm 103:4). He is a God who is forgiving and a God of healing who wants to redeem our lives from destruction.

**REFLECTION**

*How does God reveal His character?*

When we respond to God's offer of reconciliation, a marvelous transformation occurs. We become a new creation in Jesus Christ. There is an indescribable miracle that happens inside of us as we live by faith in Jesus. Faith is believing and trusting in God and God alone. It's not a matter of "turning over a new leaf" or just changing some of our old ways of doing things. A miracle has happened inside of us and we know, by faith in the Word of God, that we are new creations.

Hebrews 1:2 asserts that God has spoken through His Son. If we want to hear from God, we will follow Jesus and observe His words. We know we are hearing God's voice when it matches the character and words of Jesus. By learning the character of God, we are able to know and "hear" the way in which we should go. What a wonderful example to follow!

# Check Your Gauges!

Sometimes God seems to be silent in our lives because we are not checking our three gauges regularly. Let me (Larry) explain.

Some years back, our daughter Katrina and I had the dubious experience of destroying the engines in both of our cars on the same day. I had become so busy, that I forgot to check the oil in the vehicles. Both our cars' engines overheated and were ruined beyond repair. Since that time, I learned the extreme importance of keeping a close watch on the critical gauges on the dashboards of our cars!

We believe that, like the gauges in our cars, God has given three specific personal gauges to measure our passion for Jesus and hear His voice clearly. This enables us to maintain a proper life balance so we do not burn out in the process. These gauges include our spirit gauge, our soul gauge and our body gauge. When these gauges are all healthy, we can run the race of life for Christ to its entirety, not dropping out prematurely.

> Like the gauges in our cars, three personal gauges measure how we are living passionately for Jesus and hear His voice clearly.

As 1 Thessalonians 5:23 says, "May God himself, the God of peace, sanctify you through and through. May your whole spirit, soul and body be kept blameless at the coming of our Lord Jesus Christ."

First, we have our "spirit gauge." Jesus, our divine model, lived a life of radical obedience to the Father. In John 8:28 Jesus said, "When you have lifted up the Son of Man, then you will know that I am he and that I do nothing on my own but speak just what the Father has taught me." Jesus valued time alone with his heavenly Father, listening to his voice. Time alone with our heavenly Father each day keeps us healthy in our spirit. Let's check our spirit gauge. Are we spending proper time with our heavenly father each day?

Second, we have our "soul gauge." The enemy knows that if he can wound or make us tired in our soul, he can minimize the effect the Holy Spirit will have in our lives. Our soul—our mind, will, and emotions—needs to be cleansed and revitalized regularly. Is there anyone you have bitterness against? Keep short accounts. "For if you forgive other people when they sin against you, your heavenly Father will also forgive you," (Matthew 6:14).

**REFLECTION**
*How can you keep your spirit healthy?*

We also need to keep our emotions healthy. Jesus spent time sitting at the lake, allowing his soul to be refreshed. I love to sit on the porch and relax by looking at the trees behind our house. I often tell LaVerne how much my soul is restored by that simple act. I also love to sit at the ocean and watch the powerful waves come crashing into the shoreline. This also restores my soul. Find a way to keep your soul healthy by checking your soul gauge.

Third, we have our "body gauge." Jesus understood that His Spirit lived in a physical body and that His body and soul needed to be taken care of. He knew when to withdraw from the crowds to rest and rejuvenate His body and soul. Eating properly and exercise can also go a long way in keeping our bodies healthy. LaVerne and I love to walk together whenever we get the opportunity amidst our travel schedules.

These three gauges need to be evaluated in our lives regularly. Perhaps you are wondering why you cannot hear the voice of God in the season you are walking. Check your gauges. When we are healthy and whole in all three gauges, we are more apt and ready to hear what God wants to say to us. If any of these three areas of our lives is depleted, it will probably affect the other two areas. Check your gauges. It could save your life.

# CHAPTER 7

# Beware of the 12 D's of the Devil

**KEY MEMORY VERSE**

The thief comes only to steal
and kill and destroy;
I have come that they may have life,
and have it to the full.

John 10:10

## DAY 1

# Unmet Expectations and the Silence of God

We meet so many believers who are struggling to hear the voice of God after experiencing the disappointment of unmet expectations. They had a specific expectation for something they desired and prayed for in their lives, their family, their church or their work, but it did not happen. If we do not respond properly to unmet expectations, a root of bitterness will grow deep in our hearts (Hebrews 12:15). The bitterness will choke out our dreams, vision and our ability to hear God speak clearly to us.

When God seems to be silent, we need to guard our hearts, so that the enemy does not deceive us. The enemy is misleading many in the body of Christ today. His purpose is to eventually destroy our families, marriages, bodies, ministries and God-given destiny.

We are convinced there are twelve subtle steps the devil tries to lead us through to destroy us. We call these The 12 D's of the Devil: Disappointment, Discontentment, Discouragement, Doubt, Disbelief, Disillusionment, Deception, Disobedience, Discord, Dysfunction, Despair and Destruction. In this chapter, we will examine how these D's penetrate our lives and how we can gain victory over them. It all starts with experiencing disappointment.

1. **Disappointment:** Disappointments come from unmet expectations in our lives. These could be expectations of

what we believed God would do for us or expectations we had of our spouse, church, children or Christian leaders. It could even be expectations we have had of ourselves. The list goes on and on, but it all starts with the disappointment of unmet expectations.

Proverbs 13:12 describes the pain of unfulfilled expectations, "Hope deferred makes the heart sick." Like the writer of this proverb, many believers experience the pain of longing for something that forever seems out of reach. One of the main hindrances to living a victorious Christian life happens when our wants and needs—our expectations—are threatened. If we do not clearly disclose our desires and expectations to those involved, we will resent it when they fail to meet our needs or understand us. Perhaps we voiced our expectations, but they were ignored, dismissed or outright defied. It is in those times that the heart feels sick and it starts to affect the way we relate to others and to God.

> LaVerne and I are convinced there are twelve subtle steps the devil tries to lead us through to destroy us.

We must forgive others because the Lord has forgiven us. Remember, forgiving does not mean that what the person did was right, but forgiveness releases both parties to experience the Lord's intervention in our lives. We should respond to the unmet expectations in ways that create solutions. Ask the Lord to give you the desire and willingness to release your expectations of yourself and others, not to insist on your own way, and to be willing to find middle ground and adjust

Unmet expectations initially cause disappointment but can quickly expand into anger, hurt, helplessness and low self-esteem. If

**REFLECTION**
*What is an unmet expectation?*

we forgive, release and apply the grace of God to our lives, we will receive grace from the Lord and find our steps to freedom. But if we do not forgive, we will soon begin experiencing discontentment and fall into the trap of the 12 D's of the devil.

## DAY 2

## The Initial Stages

"The road by my house was in bad condition after a rough winter," someone wrote. "Every day I dodged potholes on the way to work. So I was relieved to see a construction crew working on the road one morning. Later, on my way home, I noticed no improvement. But where the construction crew had been working stood a new, bright-yellow sign with the words 'Rough Road.'"

As we travel through life, it may seem as if the repairs for which we petitioned God are not happening anytime soon. Instead our life is filled with rough spots. This is normal. Every person travels through rough times, and we do not need to be to be devastated by them. If we take our broken disappointment to God, He will give us the ability to navigate them. But if we allow bitterness to take root, we face an onslaught from the 12 D's of the Devil.

Recognizing, renouncing and resisting the "12 D's of the Devil" is critical in the life of every believer. Again, the key scripture this entire biblical concept is built upon is Hebrews 12:15: "See to it that no one misses the grace of God and that no bitter root grows up to cause trouble and defile many."

During any of the twelve stages, we can receive grace from the Lord to find steps to freedom. We can go back to the first stage of disappointment and choose to forgive, release and walk in freedom. When people review these twelve stages, they can usually determine the phase they are experiencing. This is helpful so that they can find freedom in the grace of God.

**Why do good people fall into horrible sin and make terrible decisions?**

So then, what is the plan of the enemy to keep us from fulfilling our destiny? And why do good people fall into horrible sin and make terrible decisions? In many cases, it is directly related to these 12 D's of the devil. This whole process does not happen overnight, but slowly, not unlike the proverbial frog dropped into a kettle of cold water that is heated so slowly that the frog doesn't realize he is being boiled.

If we face disappointment but immediately forgive, release and apply the grace of God to our lives, we will not experience steps two through twelve. But if we do not forgive and receive the grace of God, we soon begin experiencing the second stage.

2. **Discontentment**: We become negative. We stop seeing the positive in our lives and in the lives of others. Those around us may see the glass as half full while we still see it as half empty. When we enter into negativity, we may find it much harder to trust God and others. Perhaps a prayer was not answered in the way we had thought it should be answered. Again, if we apply the Word of God to our lives, walk in freedom in Christ, and go back to stage one and forgive, we get a fresh start. If not, we will soon experience stage three.

3. **Discouragement:** When we enter into the stage of discouragement, we wake up dreading the day ahead. We question whether or not life is really worth it. We feel like staying in bed and pulling the covers over our heads. Things we enjoyed in the past lose our zeal and passion. Unless we face the root of our problem, which in most cases takes us back to stage one, we will soon enter into stage four.

**REFLECTION**

*What is the key scripture that this revelation of the 12 D's of the devil is built on?*

4. **Doubt:** This takes us into the danger zone. It is in this stage that we become cynical and question everything. Sometimes we are shocked by our own doubt but the emotion feels so strong within us. Things that were completely settled in our hearts in the past are now questioned. The Bible tells us that without faith, it is impossible to please God (Hebrews 11:6). Consequently doubt opens doors that threaten our spiritual journey and relationship with the Lord.

*stop pg 5 7-21-2015*

## The Process Continues

**DAY 3**

Doubt opens doors to the following four "D's of the Devil." Keep your heart and mind open to hear from the Lord on whether you may be in any of the phases of the enemy's deception.

5. **Disbelief:** Disbelief, or unbelief, is the final form of doubt. We have trouble believing anyone. Some theological seminaries are filled with unbelief, all starting with someone in leadership who experienced unmet expectations and stopped believing the truth of the Bible. These same seminaries that were founded on the truth of the Word of God are now producing church leaders who no longer believe in the authority of the Scriptures. It's no wonder that in many places the church has lost its power! Again, if we apply the Word of God to our lives, we can walk in freedom in Christ, and go

back to stage one and forgive. Here we get a fresh start. Otherwise, we will soon experience stage six.

6. **Disillusionment:** During this stage, we have feelings of wanting to quit. It doesn't seem worth it to continue with your marriage, with a ministry, or with your church or occupation. You feel totally confused and you have lost your God-given vision. You feel like you are in a dark hole and unless you take steps to find freedom, you will set yourself up for stage number seven.

7. **Deception:** When you enter into the stage of deception, you begin to believe lies about yourself and about others. Those who are deceived do not know they are deceived. This is the essence of deception. Deception almost always starts with an unmet expectation somewhere in our lives. This small seed of deception sprouts and roots begin to grow. Most cults that deceive millions started out with a leader who experienced some type of disappointment. This disappointment grew through these stages, until the person who was disappointed initially became deceived, and in turn deceived many others. Unless we deal with the root issue of our problem, which in most cases takes us back to stage one, we will soon enter into stage eight.

> Those who are deceived do not know they are deceived. This is the essence of deception.

8. **Disobedience:** When we disobey the living God by living in disobedience to His word, we will eventually enter into a stage of living with bitterness (Hebrews 12:15). When we are bitter, we will experience both the sin of omission and the sin of commission. Disobedience to the scriptures is sin.

Many who live in disobedience think they are living an accomplished, upright life, because they are following the spiritual teaching of a

**REFLECTION**
*Have you found yourself among any of the 12 D's of the devil? If so, which ones?*

popular spiritual guru. But if these teachings contradict the Word of God, the Bible teaches that the wages of sin is death and destruction. This eventually leads to the final stage of the devil's plan for our lives.

Unless you take the steps to find freedom, you will be set up to experience further stages of the devil's strategy to kill, steal and destroy. Don't allow disbelief, disillusionment, deception and disobedience to lead you further from the beautiful plans that God has for you.

# The Enemy's Sinister Plan

We have come to the last four stages of the enemy's plan for destruction in your life. Our sincere hope is that you do not find yourself in the midst of any of these last four phases, but if you do, do not be discouraged! As we have continuously said, there is freedom for the taking! We may not be hearing from God because our hearts and mind are filled with disbelief, disobedience, doubt, discontentment and much more. We can be certain that when we choose freedom from these areas of misunderstanding, the Lord can do a great work in our lives.

9.  **Discord** When we are no longer living by the Word of God or being directed by the Holy Spirit, we will have major areas of discord in our lives. Again and again, the plots of Hollywood movies center on discord between fathers and sons, husbands and wives, and brothers and sisters. Some-times, writers, who are experiencing these very things in their own personal lives, write these scripts. When we are in this stage, there will be major people issues, broken relationships and more. It all started with those subtle unmet expectations and disappointment. Here is the good news: As long as there is life, there is hope. We can go back to stage one, forgive and receive a fresh start. If we do not, we are headed for stage number ten.

> Those whose lives and ministries have been destroyed by the devil have, in most cases, walked through these twelve stages of the devil's plan.

10. **Dysfunction:** Dysfunction takes on many forms. You can be entirely functional in one area of life and completely dysfunctional in another. Those who get to

this stage may find dysfunction in their personal lives, their marriages, their places of employment or their areas of ministry. Most dysfunction in the workplace comes from individuals who are dysfunctional. When we are dysfunctional, confusion abounds and causes miscommunication. We find ourselves going through the motions while looking for a way out, but if left unchecked, this will usher us into the eleventh stage.

11. **Despair:** When you enter into the stage of despair, you lose all hope. It is at this point that some enter into deep depression. Others have thoughts of suicide. The call and destiny of God that is on your life is completely detoured and will continue to be so until you make a decision to get back on the right road. Remember, there is always hope. There are signs all over the place, pointing you back to the main road. For those who do not follow these signs to freedom, their lot will be the final stage of the devil's plan for our lives.

12. **Destruction:** What a daunting word! Jesus tells us clearly in John 10:10, "The thief comes only to steal and kill and destroy;

**REFLECTION**
*Have you recognized any of these 12 D's of the devil in anyone's life?*

I have come that they may have life, and have it to the full." This is the place where our God-given vision, ministry or destiny can be completely destroyed by the devil. His plan is utter destruction! The final form of destruction is physical, emotional and spiritual death. Those whose lives and ministries have been destroyed by the devil have, in most cases, walked through these twelve stages of the devil's plan that was strategically laid out for them by the enemy. The sad truth is that they could have walked off the path of the enemy at any time, gone back to stage one, chose to forgive in Jesus' name, and received grace and freedom to go on and fulfill their destiny.

Always remember what it says in Romans 8:28, "And we know that in *all* things God works for the good of those who love him, who have been called according to His purpose." We serve a God who loves to redeem, restore, renew and reclaim. He will take everything we have been through and use it for good to fulfill His purposes. Remember, He is God. He can do that!

Jesus said, "I have come that they may have life, and have it to the full." Let's live life to the fullest today, and refuse to fall for the 12 D's of the devil.

## The Bell Theory

At times in our lives, we cannot hear the voice of the Lord due to our unforgiveness. The scriptures tell us that if we do not forgive others, God cannot forgive us (Matthew 6:14-15).

Some time ago, I (Larry) went to a friend who I trusted and opened my heart to him. He helped me to forgive those who I felt had hurt me, to obtain God's forgiveness and receive healing in my emotions and memories.

I found strength to go on, but to my dismay, I still dealt with the painful emotions of what had happened even though I had forgiven those who offended me and received prayer. What about James 5:16? "Therefore confess your sins to each other and pray for each other so that you may be healed." But every morning I awoke with the pain of these memories. The process of complete healing did not happen overnight, but I did find a secret to finding freedom from the painful memories.

I discovered the bell theory. I read that Corrie Ten Boom, who had experienced life in a Nazi concentration camp, learned

> Corrie Ten Boon's example helped me realize that even though the emotional pain does not immediately cease, it will grow fainter and fainter as we forgive others and thank God daily for His healing and restoration.

a spiritual principle through the analogy of a church bell. Corrie said that when you forgive someone and ask the Lord to heal and restore you, the devil tries to bring back the old emotions and memories of hurt and pain again and again. But like the final clang of a bell, the reverberations grow softer and softer until you can no longer hear the sound. Her example helped me realize that even though the emotional pain does not immediately cease, it will grow fainter and fainter as we forgive others and thank God daily for His healing and restoration.

I remembered the end portion of that same verse in James that says, "The prayer of a righteous person is powerful and effective." So every day when I awakened and remembered the painful memory, I verbally reminded myself, "I already forgave and received healing of the memories—I am free in Jesus' name." The memories lessened each day until the turmoil they provoked was gone. I still remember the incident, but the painful emotions are completely erased. Instead, I strongly sense the grace and healing of God in that area of my life.

The same holds true in forgiving ourselves.

"Two of my children lost their lives because of my *choice* to abort them," said a woman who lives in our city. "Although I knew that Jesus' blood paid for this horrible sin and redeemed the life of my children and my life, I continued to suffer in silence for many years. I continued to carry the shame and guilt of my sin."

**REFLECTION**

*Why do we need to forgive others?*

Shame causes us to hide from God. We can't hear him talking because we are too ashamed to draw close enough to hear his voice. Shame humiliates us. A litany of voices runs rampant in our minds saying, "We've blown it. We don't deserve forgiveness."

Like the woman who had the abortions, some people experience the silence of God because they can't forgive themselves for wrong decisions. 1 Peter 3:18 says, "For Christ died for sins once for all, the righteous for the unrighteous, to bring you to God. He was put to death in the body but made alive by the Spirit." Although God cleanses us from sin immediately when we ask Him, it's often a process to learn how to apply His complete forgiveness to our lives. Begin the process by renewing your mind with scripture. Gather other believers around you, those who have learned to walk in the forgiveness of God.

God will renew you as you forgive in Jesus' name, receive His healing from the painful memories, and daily thank Him for what he has already done in your life. The bell theory will help you experience complete freedom from painful memories.

# Unfulfilled Dreams

DAY 6

Some months ago, I was ministering in Europe. The next week I was in the Caribbean and the next in the United States. I experienced three different parts of the world within three weeks, but I saw amazing similarities. Three cultures, same Jesus. Three regions, same kingdom. Three churches, same heart to experience all that the Lord has for each of them. Yet in each nation, I also met people who experienced unfulfilled dreams.

LaVerne and I find ourselves drawn to those who are experiencing the deep disappointment of unfulfilled dreams, because we have walked many times in those shoes. We've discovered that when we really understand the ways and processes of our God, we can see that unfulfilled dreams become a part of the Lord's strategy. He desires to get us to where we can know Him more intimately and where we are the most fruitful.

Jesus said it like this: "unless a grain of wheat falls into the ground and dies, it remains alone; but if it dies, it produces much grain" (John 12:24). Sometimes our present understanding of our dreams needs to die so the Lord can fulfill them in His way and in His time. The disciples thought it was all over when Jesus went to the cross, but it was only the beginning! Like the disciples, we find that God often fulfills our unfulfilled dreams in amazing ways that are above what we can dream or imagine.

> We've discovered that when we really understand the ways and processes of our God, we can see that unfulfilled dreams become a part of the Lord's strategy.

Many times we have mentored younger Christian leaders with much potential for leadership who have taken a different path in their lives. LaVerne and I came to realize that even though we had a dream for them, this may not have been God's dream for them. We have also served believers who have lost their faith, choosing to live an ungodly lifestyle rather than following the Lord and

His purposes. It is devastating to see those with so much potential wasting their lives. But God reminds us that the last chapter has not yet been written.

Sometimes our focus needs to shift. It is easy to concentrate upon the dreams in our heart that have not come to pass. Psalm 39:7 says, "But now, Lord, what do I look for? My hope is in you." Many people use the phrase, "I hope so," but this relates more to the thought of "wishful thinking." God offers us true hope. As we grow in maturity within our faith, we begin to understand the character of God. God is hope. As it says in Romans 15:13, it is our God of hope who fills us with joy and peace as we trust in Him, not our circumstances. The focus of our hope must be Jesus.

Even Paul faced despair in regards to circumstances in his life. But he says in 2 Corinthians 1:9-10 that "Indeed, in our hearts we felt the sentence of death. But this happened that we might not rely on ourselves but on God, who raises the dead. He has delivered us from such a deadly peril, and he will deliver us. On him we have set our hope that he will continue to deliver us."

Paul made a choice to set his hope on Jesus, not on his current condition.

**REFLECTION**

*What unfulfilled dreams do you have?*

Hope is trusting that His promises are true. He has a plan for you. It is a plan to prosper you and not to harm you. A plan to give you a hope and a future (Jeremiah 29:11). Surrender your disappointment from your unfulfilled dreams to the Lord. Watch and see how a shift in focus and attitude opens up the door for the Lord to do a work within you. It will be better than anything you could have dreamed!

Allow the Lord to take you and your broken, unfulfilled dreams to the cross, and He will mold them into His dreams. You will become more intimate with Him. In the process, you will experience His grace and strength. He will work in you above all you can ask or think.

## Beware of the Counterfeit

The enemy of your soul does not want you to hear from the Lord! As you endeavor to listen for God's voice, the devil may discourage you by placing traps. You are in warfare against the powers of darkness. Do not take this lightly! Let's look at some of the traps to be aware of as you listen for God's voice.

We read in 2 Timothy 4:3-4, "that in the last days, many false prophets will rise up and tell people what their ears want to hear. People will gravitate toward teachers who tell them something pleasing and gratifying. To suit their own desires, they will turn away from hearing the truth and will wander off into listening to myths and man-made fictions."

Today television shows feature psychics who claim to be connecting with the spiritual realm of departed loved ones. These mediums communicate with "familiar spirits" who tell half-truths about the past and fabricate the future. God's Word clearly tells us, "Turn not to those [mediums] who have familiar spirits or to wizards; do not seek them out to be defiled by them. I am the Lord your God" (Leviticus 19:31). The seriousness of entertaining familiar spirits (a type of evil spirit) is plainly set forth in God's Word. Spiritualism, witchcraft and divination are all forbidden in the Word of God.

Some Christians read horoscopes and consult psychics and question why they do not have peace in their lives! They are walking in deception. Our faith must be in God alone. As believers in Jesus Christ, we do not depend on luck or the predictions of a psychic, but on the grace of God and His ability to bless us.

> The seriousness of entertaining familiar spirits (a type of evil spirit) is plainly set forth in God's Word.

The enemy will scheme to keep you from hearing from God and even create a counterfeit. Did you ever get one of those "Christian" chain emails with inspirational stories that say if you really love God, you must pass it along to ten people you care about within 48 hours? Forwarding an email will not prove your love for God. These emails are no different than those that predict bad luck if they are not forwarded. By deceiving us with superstitions motivated by false guilt, Satan tries to counterfeit God's voice in our lives. We must counter these schemes with the Word of God that clearly says the Holy Spirit dwells inside of each one of us and will lead us individually. Entrusting ourselves into the hands of our loving Father will help us develop an ability to hear and be led by His Spirit.

God's voice will be distorted if you place something or someone ahead of Him. The prophet Ezekiel tells how the elders of Israel came to him to get information about the future, but God saw their idolatrous hearts and answered them according to their idols (Ezekiel 14:1-5).

Let us explain. If you come to God asking Him for something that you have not submitted to Him inwardly, it becomes an idol in your heart. If the "thing" or desire is held more prominently in your consciousness than Jesus, your answer will return tainted. God may give you an answer as delusive as the idol you are entertaining in your heart. He may answer your prayer and give you what you want, but you will later regret it. The children of Israel grumbled, and the Lord gave them what they wanted, but they ate quail until they could not stand it any more!

**REFLECTION**
*What are some counterfeits of the Holy Spirit's work?*

The Bible speaks of a highway of holiness on which we are to walk, and that "whoever walks the road, although a fool, shall not go astray" (Isaiah 35:8). Let us learn to resist the enemy's schemes that keep us from hearing the Lord's voice clearly.

*9-7-2015*

# Embracing the Journey

# The Dark Night of the Soul

If we are experiencing a time of God's silence, we are not alone. Jesus understands how we feel. He cried out in anguish on the cross, "My God, my God why have you forsaken me"? (Matthew 27:46). This experience sometimes is called the dark night of the soul.

We should not fear God's silence nor the dark night of the soul, because it is a reminder that we need Him desperately. When He is silent and life seems dark, it often motivates us to place our full trust in God. Think about it. When we are lost in the woods, we pay more attention to directions. God may be building our character to cause us to be more effective in His kingdom. In the darkness of God's silence, we are reminded of what we are missing.

Writer Paul Thigpen says that the deepest sorrows and the highest joys are best shared in silence:

"I remember two quiet, wordless moments that reflected this truth in my own life. One took place when I stood silently by my father's casket at his funeral. The other came when I stood watching my firstborn child, only a few moments old, and wept silently over the miracle that had made me a father."[1]

God is sometimes silent because words will distract from the love and care He is trying to convey to us in His quietness. Zephaniah, the prophet, describes this silence of love: "He will be quiet in His love" (Zephaniah 3:17). If you are going through a time in your life where God seems distant, pray for wisdom to interpret the silence. Whether He is silent to test you or quiet you in His love, He always intends that you put your trust in Him. This is so that He can do a deep work in you. You can trust Him.

When God is silent, it doesn't mean that He is absent. King David, on more than one occasion, felt abandoned by God. Yet despite the silence, David knew he was never out of God's sight. In the Psalms, David referred to this truth again and again. He asks in Psalm 139, "Where can I go from your Spirit: Where can I flee from your presence? . . . If I settle on the far side of the sea, even there your hand will guide me, your right hand will hold me fast. . . ."

> When God is silent, it doesn't mean that He is absent.

Listen to Isaiah's words in chapter 30, verse 15, about God waiting for us in His silence. "This is what the Sovereign Lord, the Holy One of Israel, says: 'In repentance and rest is your salvation, in quietness and trust is your strength.'" Isaiah goes on to say in verse 18, "the Lord must wait for you to come to him so he can show you his love and compassion . . . blessed are those who wait for his help." What a wonderful promise to us! When God is silent, we must choose to trust His silence, quiet ourselves and wait on Him.

At some point, everyone goes through these seasons of the dark night of the soul. Some people admit it and others do not, but LaVerne and I are convinced that everyone experiences these times of God's silence. We have found that during these times we grow closer to the Lord more than at any other time. We are being trained and positioned by the Lord to help others, who will be facing seasons of God's silence in their lives. We will completely empathize because we have been there ourselves. We will not tell

**REFLECTION**

*Describe a time when God seemed silent but you knew He was still there*

them to get their act together, but in deep humility, point them to Jesus, the author and finisher of our faith. He will pour His life into them and give them strength. The Lord will be glorified.

Let's embrace this season.

## DAY 2 | Consolation and Desolation

Author Thomas F. Fischer explains the dark night of the soul in another way. He speaks of "consolation and desolation" that he learned from the church fathers in The Spiritual Exercises of St. Ignatius (1491-1556). "Consolation," Ignatius wrote, is when "the soul is aroused by an interior movement which causes it to be inflamed with love of its creator and Lord. . . ."[1]

"Desolation" in stark contrast to "consolation" is defined as the "darkness of the soul, turmoil of the mind, inclination to low and earthly things, restlessness resulting from many disturbances and temptations which lead to loss of faith, loss of hope, and loss of love. It is also desolation when a soul finds itself completely apathetic, tepid, sad and separated as it were from its Creator and Lord."

> Perhaps the most profound advice for those in desolation is found in Ignatius' focus on "sufficient grace."

Ignatius gives us advice and strategies to help us during times of desolation.

1. When in desolation, stay the course.

2. In desolation, remember God is really there.

3. The most important thing in desolation is patience.

4. In desolation, think long-term.

5. Starve desolation with increased spirituality.

6. Use times of consolation wisely, including planning ahead for the next desolation.

7. Know the enemy.

8. Consider the reasons for your desolation.

Fischer tells us that not all trials and desolation are created equal. Ignatius notes three reasons we may be in desolation. (1) Because of our own negligence of spiritual discipline. (2) God is testing how we will respond when the result is desolation and not an expected reward. (3) God wishes to impart special wisdom and spiritual understanding. If such insight were attained apart from desolation, Ignatius noted that it would allow "our intellect to rise up in a spirit of pride or vainglory."

Perhaps the most profound advice for those in desolation is found in Ignatius' focus on sufficient grace. "A person who is in desolation should recall that he can do much to withstand all of his enemies by using the sufficient grace that he has, and taking strength in his Creator and Lord."

Sufficient grace reminds us of Paul's words in 2 Corinthians 12:9-10, "My grace is sufficient for you, for my power is made perfect in weakness." Therefore I will boast all the more gladly about my weaknesses, so that Christ's power may rest on me. That is why, for Christ's sake, I delight in weaknesses, in insults, in hardships, in persecutions, in difficulties. For when I am weak, then I am strong."

God's grace is truly sufficient for us when we walk through any valley. David said it well in Psalm 23, "Even when I walk through the darkest valley, I will not be afraid,

**REFLECTION**
*What is the difference between consolation and desolation?*

for you are close beside me. Your rod and your staff protect and comfort me. You prepare a feast for me in the presence of my enemies. You honor me by anointing my head with oil. My cup overflows with blessings" (Psalm 23:4, 5).

10-5-2015
8:30 Pm

# Surprised by His Voice

Anyone who is in a long-distant relationship knows that hearing a friend's voice over the telephone is a welcomed sound. Fresh communication is important for any relationship. God will sometimes surprise us through an unexpected revelation from Him. By now, it should not surprise us that God uses many options to speak to us.

Sometimes God surprises us and speaks in a way we would never expect. For example, there is a story in the Bible in the book of Numbers chapter 22 when the Lord spoke through a donkey to the prophet Balaam. At the time, Balaam was out of the will of God and trying to walk through a door the Lord had closed to him. The Lord sent an angel to block Balaam and his donkey from continuing forward and the donkey saw the angel, but Balaam did not. That is, until he beat the donkey to try to make it

> It should not surprise us that God uses many, many options to speak to us.

move, and the Lord caused the donkey to talk! Not only were Balaam's ears opened, but his eyes were opened as well. He saw an angel with a sword drawn in the path. God rebuked the greedy prophet in this unusual way to keep him from making a serious mistake. Sometimes God's surprises will keep us from making the wrong move in our lives.

*Larry Came + Talked with our small group. 1-2-2015*

Although rare, God may even surprise us by speaking through an audible voice. On occasion, God's people in both the Old and New Testaments heard His literal, audible words. We know about Adam, with whom God walked and talked in the Garden of Eden. God also spoke audibly to the prophets and the patriarchs such as Noah. In the New Testament, Peter, James and John heard God's voice during the transfiguration. In Acts 9, at Paul's conversion on the Damascus road, Christ spoke directly to Paul, and those around him also heard Jesus speaking.

However, it is interesting to note, that although the Acts 9 account mentions that others also heard, when Paul is describing his conversion experience in a later chapter, he says those with him "saw the light but did not hear the voice of the One who was speaking to me." Bible scholars attribute this seeming contradiction to the Greek translation of the word "hear." In the first account, the Greek word used actually means they "heard something without understanding." When Paul describes his experience later, he uses the Greek word that means that those with him did not "discern" the voice of the Lord. They heard the sound, but couldn't make out what was being said.

A similar occurrence takes place when Jesus was teaching one day and God spoke audibly. Although the disciples heard God's audible voice and understood exactly what He spoke, some people heard God's voice as "thunder" and some thought an angel had spoken. How could people hear the same voice but hear it differently? Could it be that it depended on the spiritual state of the person hearing? Not everyone was in a spiritual position to hear the voice as God's and some probably thought it was just their imaginations running wild.

**REFLECTION**

*In Numbers 22, a donkey talked for God! Did God ever speak to you in an unusual or unexpected way?*

It is important for us not only to hear but also to hear with understanding. It is quite possible that to hear God's audible voice, we must be in a position to hear it. Our hearts must be open to hear Him, just as little Samuel's was when he finally recognized the voice he was hearing as God's. Samuel responded in childlike faith, "Speak, I'm listening." In other words, it is easier to discern God's voice when we are in a close relationship with the Lord, like Samuel, who "continually ministered before the Lord." Stay close to Him because even in the seeming silence, His audible voice could surprise you!

## Touched By an Angel

Even when we do not seem to be hearing God speak clearly, according to the Bible, we have angels looking out for us. God created angels to help accomplish His work in this world, and they watch over and assist us, because we belong to God. This is amazing but true.

Psalm 91:11 says, "For he will command his angels concerning you to guard you in all your ways."

Former President Ronald Reagan's daughter relates the story of visiting her father in the hospital, soon after someone tried to assassinate him. Apparently, he saw angels surrounding him during this critical time after surgery.

"My mother told me that he woke up at one point after the doctors had operated on him, unable to talk because there was a tube down his throat. He saw figures in white standing around him and scrawled on a piece of paper, 'I'm alive, aren't I?' . . . I repeated [the story] to a friend—a nurse—who pointed out to me that no one in a recovery room or in intensive care is in white; they're all in green scrubs. . . . I give endless prayers of thanks to whatever angels circled my father, because a devastator bullet, which miraculously had not exploded, was finally found a quarter inch from his heart. Without divine intervention, I don't know if he would have survived."

> Just because you have never seen an angel does not mean angels are not present with you.

When Peter was released from prison by an angel and arrived at the door of Mary's house in Acts chapter 10, the believers meeting there could not believe Peter had arrived in person. They said, "It must be his [guardian] angel." Angels appeared throughout the Bible. I believe angels often are present today. Jesus had told His followers earlier that those with childlike faith would have the services of angels, "their angels have constant access to my Father" (Matthew 18:10).

As a believer, God provides angels for you because He loves you and He will speak comfort and protection to you through these messengers. You may not be aware of the presence of angels around you. You cannot predict how they will appear, for the Bible says, "Do not forget to entertain strangers, for by so doing some people have entertained angels without knowing it" (Hebrews 13:2).

Just because you have never seen an angel does not mean angels are not present with you. LaVerne is convinced that I have many angels who protect me while I drive, because I often get so preoccupied while driving that I need supernatural intervention to keep the car on the road!

Seriously, angels are spirits that make themselves visible when needed. There have been angelic sightings all over the world. We have a close relative who saw an angel in her bedroom. The angel brought her comfort and hope during a time of great need. She said that a deep peace came over her when she had the angelic visitation.

**REFLECTION**
*Have you ever experienced an angelic encounter?*

A friend of ours was detained in Albania for handing out Bibles when that nation had a strict communist regime. Amazingly, she and her friend were released. The problem was that they were released in the middle of nowhere, each with a heavy suitcase and it was miles to the Yugoslavian border. Miraculously, a man stopped and offered to drive them through the countryside and straight to the border. After he had dropped them off, he disappeared by returning the way he had come. These friends are convinced the man was an angel who provided help for them.

When God seems silent, open up your eyes! Remember that He has His angels watching and guarding over you. You are protected. Our God loves to surprise us. You may encounter an angel even if you do not recognize one. Let's stay ready for whatever angelic encounter the Lord may be using to speak to us in our time of need. God may seem to be silent at times, but his angels are watching out for us.

*Stopped 11-16-2015*

## Look to See What He Will Say

DAY 5

Sometimes we are listening for a voice when God is trying to talk to us through those around us. One day Jesus said: "I tell you the truth, the Son can do nothing by himself; he can do only what he sees his Father doing, because whatever the Father does the Son also does" (John 5:19). This means that we can "hear" with our eyes. For example, we communicate to our children by the way we model our lives. Our God often speaks to us by what we see Him doing among us.

We must be careful not to assume that God will speak to us in only one particular way. Look around and see how He is working and learn to recognize the activity of God.

The prophet Habakkuk said, "I will look to see what he will say to me" (Habakkuk 2:1). Many times that which God is saying to us is right in front of us! I know that if LaVerne is overwhelmed with a busy schedule and needs a break, I don't need an angelic visitation in order to give her a break or to encourage her to rest. When we want to give our opinion or counsel to someone the Lord has placed into our lives, we should keep our spiritual eyes open. The Father is always doing something, and we can easily miss it. We must find out what He is saying to those around us.

> When I pray with people who are going through deep waters, I often keep my eyes open to see what the Father is doing within them as I pray.

When I (LaVerne) pray with people who are going through deep waters, I often keep my eyes open to see what the Father is doing within them as I pray. If the person begins to show emotion and cry, I may change the way I am praying, because I am following what I see the Father doing.

In *Experiencing God*, Henry Blackaby describes a time his church sensed that God was leading them into outreach ministry to the college campus. For two years they held Bible studies in the dorms, but with no results. Pastor Blackaby finally pulled the church's students aside and said, "This week I want you to go to the campus and watch to see where God is working and join Him." He explained further, "No one will ask after spiritual matters unless God is at work in his life. When you see someone seeking God or asking about spiritual matters, you are seeing God at work. If someone starts asking you spiritual questions, whatever else you have planned, don't do it. Cancel what you are doing. Go with that individual and look to see what God is doing there.

"On Wednesday one of the girls reported, 'Oh, Pastor, a girl who has been in classes with me for two years came to me after class today. She said, "I think you might be a Christian. I need to talk to you." I remembered what you said. I had a class, but I missed it. We went to the cafeteria to talk. She said, 'Eleven of us girls have been studying the Bible, and none of us are Christians. Do you know somebody who can lead us in a Bible study?' As a result of that contact, we started three Bible study groups in the women's dorms and two in the men's dorm. For two years we tried to do something for God and failed. For three days we looked to see where God was working and joined Him. What a difference that made!"[1]

We should be willing to trust and have faith in God even when we do not understand His ways.

**REFLECTION**

*What does it mean to look to see what He will say?*

The way God thinks is far beyond the way we think, from a natural perspective. "As the heavens are higher than the earth, so are my ways higher than your ways and my thoughts than your thoughts" (Isaiah 55:9). But God invites us to learn His way. That's why we should intentionally listen for His voice and adjust our lives to Him in obedience. Just think, our breakthrough could come from simply opening our eyes, seeing how He is working and choosing to act upon it! Let's not limit the way we experience His voice.

## He Is the God of the Process

The Lord is much more concerned about what He is doing in us than having us reach our goals. He wants us to depend on Him and His power in the here and now. Oswald Chambers said, "If I can stay calm, faithful and unconfused while in the middle of the turmoil of life, the goal of the purpose of God is being accomplished in me. God is not working toward a particular finish—His purpose is the process itself." God's silence will reveal our true attitudes toward God by showing us what is really in our hearts and giving us the opportunity to fully trust in His power.

God may be silent due to no fault of our own, because He is simply developing within us depth of character and deeper trust in Him. At other times, He may be silent due to our disobedience. King David said, "If I had not confessed the sin in my heart, my Lord would not have listened" (Psalm 66:18). Sin alienates us from God and creates a barrier to hearing from Him. In times like these, God's silences may be an act of judgment.

In the days of Samuel the prophet, the priests were ungodly men, and the Bible says "the word of the Lord was rare." God refused to speak because these rebellious priests misrepresented God to the people. Because they didn't hear God's voice for a period of time, the people became hungry to hear it again, but God's silence paved the way for Samuel to be heard as God's spokesman. If we cannot hear God's voice, we must examine ourselves to see what could be possibly hindering us from hearing.

> A heart that is not willing to obey the Lord is a disobedient heart, and disobedience is sin.

We can learn some valuable insights on hearing from God from George Mueller, a man of faith from 19th-century England. Here are some of Mueller's suggestions:

"I seek at the beginning to get my heart in such a state that it has no will of its own in regard to a given matter. . . . Nine-tenths of the difficulties are overcome when our hearts are ready to do the Lord's will whatever it may be. . . . Having done this, I do not leave the result to feeling or simple impression. If so, I make myself liable to great delusions. I will seek the will of the Spirit of God through, or in connection with, the Word of God. . . . If the Holy Ghost guides us at all, He will do it according to the scriptures and never contrary to them. . . . Next, I take into account providential circumstances. These often plainly indicate God's will in connection with His Word and Spirit. I ask God in prayer to reveal His will to me aright. . . . Thus, through prayer to God, the study of the Word, and reflection, I come to deliberate judgment according to the best of my ability and knowledge, and if my mind is thus at peace, and continues so after two or three more petitions, I proceed accordingly. In trivial matters and in transactions involving most important issues, I find this method effective. . . . But if honesty of heart and uprightness before God were lacking, or if I did not patiently wait upon God for instruction, or if I preferred the counsel of my fellow man to the declarations of the Word of the living God, I made great mistakes."[1]

Notice how Mueller focuses on being sure that his heart is ready to do whatever the Lord asks of him. A heart that is not willing to obey the Lord is a disobedient heart, and disobedience is sin.

Even after many years of practicing God's presence, Mr. Mueller admitted

**REFLECTION**

*Have I obeyed the last thing the Lord asked me to do?*

that he still made mistakes in hearing from God. There is no fool-proof method to hearing. But we know that God is faithful.

The psalmist directed his prayers to God expecting an answer, "In the morning I lay my requests before you and wait in expectation." God wants us to make our first petitions to Him each day as we live in expectancy of an answer. Jeremiah 33:3 says, "Call unto me and I will answer you and show you great and mighty things. . . ." When we seek God, He promises to answer—of that we can be sure. And He is teaching us perseverance as a part of His process in our lives.

## A Life of Devotion to Him

We are close to the end of our journey together in learning what to do when God seems to be silent. To sum it up, it is all about our personal relationship with our God. To walk with Him is to lead a life of devotion to Him. We know what it is for two friends to walk together, engaged in close and intimate conversation. Having a devoted relationship with someone is an adventure full of surprises.

The Bible singles out one of two men in particular by saying, "Enoch walked with God." The only other man in the entire Bible to hold this same distinction is Noah. What did Enoch do that placed him in this exclusive God-recognized category? We know little about Enoch, other than the fact that he lived for 365 years, bore Methuselah and was then translated from earth to heaven, passing over death. Apparently God honored him because he walked pleasingly before the Lord. Methuselah realized he was always under the seeing eye of God and lived a life of communion with God.

We take every opportunity to talk with our children. Why wouldn't our heavenly Father desire to do the same with us? We would not expect our children to know what we wanted them to do if we did not talk with them. So why would God feel any differently?

Jesus honored whatever His Father said, no matter what the personal cost. We will not hear the Lord's voice

> Living minute by minute in the presence of God takes practice.

clearly if we only listen to God when He tells us only what we want to hear. We must be willing to lay aside our own desires or we may miss a clear word from the Lord. Our natural inclination tends to manipulate things to work the way we want them to work. We need to be open to messages God may send through people who love us and are praying for us. God wants us to stay humble and ready to hear from Him regardless of the way He chooses to speak.

Brother Lawrence, a monk from the seventeenth century, said, "We must know before we can love. In order to know God, we must often think of Him. And when we come to love Him, we shall then also think of Him often, for our heart will be with our treasure." Brother Lawrence described this continuous practice of the presence of God as a "quiet, familiar conversation with Him."[1]

Walking in the loving presence of God daily and making each day one continuous prayer can be compared to the biblical challenge to "pray without ceasing" (1 Thessalonians 5:17). But how is it possible to fellowship with God continously? Can it become as natural as breathing? We believe it can as we learn to listen.

God longs for you to open your spiritual ears, to hear Him speak, as you walk through your daily life. How is it possible to live minute by minute in the presence of God? When you are learning a new language, at first you are insecure and uncertain; however, as you practice, you become more secure as you learn the new language's distinguishing sounds. Living minute by minute in the presence of God takes practice. We believe that practicing the presence of God can take place in the midst of your routine as you learn to tune your spirit to loving the Lord with your whole heart, soul and mind.

Hearing from God is a journey. After many years of listening for His voice, we still make mistakes in hearing clearly. Our prayer for you is that you will experience the Lord and hear His voice in a whole new dimension as you continue

**REFLECTION**
*Name some attributes of friendship. Do you have this type of friendship with God?*

your lifetime walk with Jesus. Even when He seems to be silent for a season, you will know that He is faithful and is working in your life "underground," preparing you for the days ahead. He is a good God! Together let's fulfill the Lord's purpose for our lives as we look forward to His return.

As for today, let's embrace the journey.

*Slnished the book*

*11-30-2015*
*8:15 PM*

# Endnotes

**Chapter 1, Day 6**
C. S. Lewis, *The Chronicles of Narnia* (New York: Macmillan Publishing Company, 1950).

**Chapter 2, Day 4**
Nick Vujicic, *Unstoppable: The Incredible Power of Faith in Action* (Colorado: Waterbrook Press, 2012), 106.

**Chapter 2, Day 5**
Randy Alcorn, *If God is Good* (Colorado: Multnomah Books, 2009), 212.

**Chapter 2, Day 6**
Catherine Marshall, *Light in my Darkest Night* (New York: Avon Books, 1989), 199, 205.

**Chapter 3, Day 4**
Sharon Daugherty, *Walking in the Spirit* (Oklahoma: Harrison House, 1984), 49-50.

**Chapter 5, Day 4**
A.T. Pierson, *George Mueller, His Life of Prayer and Faith* (England: 1899).

**Chapter 6, Day 3**
Cornell Haan, *Which Intercessor Most Influenced Your Prayer Life?* (Florida: Charisma House, *Charisma*, September/October 2004), 14.

**Chapter 6, Day 4**
Mark and Patti Virkler, *Communion With God* (Pennsylvania: Destiny Image Publishers, 1991).

**Chapter 8, Day 1**
Paul Thigpen, *O God, Do Not Be Silent* (Florida: Charisma House, Charisma Magazine, 1992), 59.

**Chapter 8, Day 2**
Anthony Mottola, *The Spiritual Exercises of St. Ignatius* (New York: Image Books, 1964),129-131.

(Excerpts taken from: http://www.ministryhealth.net/ mh_articles/314_ignatius_survive_desolation.html).

**Chapter 8, Day 5**
Henry Blackaby and Claude King, *Experiencing God* (Tennesee: Broadman & Holman Publishers, 1994).

**Chapter 8, Day 6**
A.T. Pierson, *George Mueller, His Life of Prayer and Faith* (England: 1899).

**Chapter 8, Day 7**
Brother Lawrence, *The Practice of the Presence of God* (Pennsylvania: Whitaker House, 1982), 49, 80

Ibid., p. 24, 80.

## When God Seems Silent
### Chapter 1 Outline

# When God Seems to Stop Speaking

## 1. When it all Falls Apart

a. When everything seems to be crumbling around us, we often believe God is silent.

b. Hurt, failure and fear smother God's voice.

c. The truth is that Hebrews 13:5 promises: "Never will I leave you; Never will I forsake you."

## 2. There is Hope

a. Bible records examples of how God works beneath the surface of people's lives during times of seemingly silences.

b. Circumstances are not necessarily the result of people or even Satan attacking us. Joseph told his brothers, "So then, it was not you who sent me here, but God."

c. God redeems our darkest hours for his good.

## 3. The Bamboo Tree Principle

a. Bamboo seedling is planted, it develops a root system that is many miles long beneath the surface enabling it to grow ninety feet in its sixth year.

b. Jesus said, "As the Father has loved me, so I also love you," (John 15:9). That scriptural truth must become more than head knowledge.

## 4. An Unfamiliar Form

a. Things had neither turned out the way the disciples wanted nor the way they were sure Jesus had promised.

b. On the road to Emmaus the disciples did not recognize the person they longed to see when He joined them on their walk and entered into conversation with them.

c. "When he was at the table, he took bread, gave thanks, broke it and began to give it to them. Then their eyes were opened and they recognized him" (Luke 24:30, 31).

## 5. Beyond the Circumstances

a. Focus on the truth of God's revealed Word in the Bible. His Word speaks life into our silence.

b. When God seems to be silent, persist in speaking the Word of God: "Nothing is too difficult for God" (Luke 1:37).

c. The results may be different than we had expected, but we can trust Him.

## 6. The Proper Voice

a. Often our soul (thoughts, will and emotions) wants something so badly that we confuse it with hearing from God.

b. Remember, God's Word and God's voice are one and the same (John 1:1).

c. Psalm 46:10 invites us to "be still and know that I am God." He is teaching us to listen for the voice of truth.

## 7. The Sun Is Still Shining

a. Our perspective of Him may be like our perspective of the sun. God is good because my life is good or vice versa.

b. Habakkuk 3:17-19 tells us: "Though the fig tree does not bud and there are no grapes in the vines, though the olive crop fails and the fields produce no food, though there are no sheep in the pen and no cattle in the stalls, yet I will rejoice in the Lord, I will be joyful in God my Savior. The Sovereign Lord is my strength, he makes my feet like the feet of a deer, and He enables me to go on the heights."

c. Remember, when He is silent, the night seems dark, and the clouds heavy, the sun is still shining above the clouds. Let us continue to be aware of that sun!

# When God Seems Silent
## Chapter 2 Outline
# Seasons

### 1. A Season for all Things
a. Many times we miss what God is trying to teach us because we are so focused on wanting instant gratification.

b. God appoints seasons of preparation for us, and seasons when our dreams come to pass. Fulfillment of our dreams is dependent on God's timing.

c. Find something of beauty in the time and season you are in; and remember, it is only for a season. If you allow it, God will use it to prepare you for your future.

d. Esther in the Bible went through a hard winter season as an orphaned child, but the Lord had been preparing her for years to be in the right place at the right time.

### 2. His Perfect Time
a. So often, during times when God seems to be silent, He is teaching us to wait until the timing is right.

*Ex: Soon-to-be mother endures.*

b. While we are waiting, we can become impatient.

*Ex: Christian businessman invests.*

### 3. The Power of Thankfulness
a. Being thankful is a decision.

*Ex: Charlie Brown's dog Snoopy...it dawns on him.*

b. Gratefulness changes us and others.

*Ex: Rwanda genocide.*

c. Even when God seems silent, the Bible instructs us to give thanks.

*Ex: Job kept an attitude of praise in turmoil.*

## 4. Keep Your Eyes on the Prize

a.  The devil knows that if he can get us to focus on failing, fear, poverty, disease or our negative circumstances, we will become defeated and depressed.

*Ex: Nick Vujicic born without limbs changes his focus.*

b.  When we surrender our circumstances to God, the blockage to hearing His voice is removed.

## 5. When We Receive Bad News

a.  Unpleasant events are opposite of what we interpret as God's goodness.

*Ex: Keith Yoder's diagnosis with cancer*

b.  Bad news forces us to examine the truth of God's Word.

*Ex: Randy Alcorn writes, "Look at Christ. He shouts to us without opening his mouth. Don't you see the blood, bruises and scars?*

## 6. Learning from Jesus and His Disciples

a.  Disciples often focused on circumstances rather than Him.

*Ex: Stormy seas*

*Ex: When the disciples saw him walking on the water.*

b.  Jesus faced God's silence on the cross.

## 7. Living in the Present

a.  Enemy tempts us to live in the past or future. God wants us to live to the fullest in the present.

*Ex: John Newton*

b.  Every miracle in the Bible was preceded by a problem. The Red Sea parting, Jesus feeding the five thousand, blind man healed.

c.  Don't miss God-given opportunities.

*Ex: Alexander Bell*

*Ex: Friend wasted time looking backward.*

## When God Seems Silent
### Chapter 3 Outline
# Taking Baby Steps

### 1. Baby Steps
    a.  Always keep praying and step out in faith.

        *Ex: What About Bob?*

    b.  The Lord leads us one step at a time.

    c.  Some of God's people spend their lives in so much fear of making a mistake that they never do anything. Listen and take steps forward, no matter how small the steps.

### 2. The God of the Second Chance
    a.  Do you feel as if you made too many mistakes? Our God is the God of the second chance.

        *Ex: "Then the word of the Lord came to Jonah a second time" (Jonah 3:1).*

    b.  God has a "track record" of using those who feel as if they cannot do the job.

        *Ex: Jeremiah*

### 3. The Fear of the Lord
    a.  A healthy understanding of the fear of the Lord is to be awestruck by His power and presence.

    b.  If we love, honor and respect our God, we will want to obey Him.

        *Ex: Francis Chan*

    c.  When we understand the fear of the Lord, we will turn from sin and trust Jesus to wash, cleanse and make us new.

**4. Rest and Retreat Can Break the Silence**

   a.  We are predisposed to believe we need to earn God's approval.

   b.  Identity is not in accomplishments, but God alone.
      *Ex: Merle Shenk.*

   c.  The clamoring of everyday living can block our ability to hear God speaking.
      *Ex: Sharon Daugherty*

**5. Start Moving**

   a.  When the motivations of our prayers are based on fear, our perspective becomes cloudy. Commit to walking through the assigned task that He has given.

   b.  Sometimes when God seems to be silent, He is waiting for us to obey what He has spoken through His Word.

**6. What We Cannot See**

   a.  Why doesn't God answer our prayers as he promised?
      *Ex. Mary and Martha when Lazarus died.*
      *Ex. Missionary's car breakdown.*

   b.  As Lazarus was taking his last breaths, little did Martha know, God was preparing a far greater miracle than healing. He was preparing a resurrection.

**7. Our Friend and Guide**

   a.  Sometimes when God is silent, He is calling us into a deeper level of friendship with Him.

   b.  John 16:12-13 says, "I have much more to say to you, more than you can now bear. But when he, the Spirit of truth, comes, he will guide you into all truth. He will not speak on his own; he will speak only what he hears, and he will tell you what is yet to come."
      *Ex. Holy Spirit is like our AAA guide.*

## When God Seems Silent
### Chapter 4 Outline
# Walking in Faith

## 1. The Power of our Words

a.  Guard the words we say to ourselves and to others. Life and death are in the power of the tongue (Proverbs 18:21).

b.  The enemy uses our words to plant fear. Job 3:25 tells us, "For the thing I greatly feared has come upon me, and what I dreaded has happened to me."

c.  With every whispered lie of the devil, the Word of God will always supercede it.

## 2. Become a Berean

a.  Focus on the truth of the Scriptures, not on man's ideas. The Bible says the Bereans "received the message with eagerness and examined the Scriptures every day to see if what Paul said was true" (Acts 17:11).

b.  The Bible is the revelation of God to humanity. Read it with the expectation that God will speak through its words.
    *Ex: Reyna Britton*

c.  The truth of God's Word will break through when God seems to be silent.

## 3. Freedom from Condemnation

a.  Sometimes we live in condemnation and shame because of wrong decisions we have made.

b.  The devil condemns. God convicts. Condemnation brings doubt, fear, unbelief, shame, and hopelessness. Conviction brings hope and a way towards freedom.
    *Ex: Oswald Chambers*

c.  Replace words and thoughts of condemnation with the truth of God's Word.

4. **Responses to Personal Criticism**
   a. Sometimes improperly processing criticism can keep us from hearing the Lord speak to us: Defend ourself, rehash it over and over, criticize the person who criticized us, tell lots of people why we are right and the offender is wrong.
   b. Use it as an impetus for change and personal growth.

5. **Looking Through History**
   a. We can learn from the experiences of others.

      *Ex Israelites complained because of the monotonous manna*
   c. By discovering how others overcame their problems help us find answers to problems.

6. **Walking in Faith**
   a. Local church provides a community of believers who interact to encourage each other to hear from God.

      *Ex: Hot coal burned brightly until withdrawn from fire.*
   b. "But encourage one another daily. . . so that none of you may be hardened by sin's deceitfulness" (Hebrews 3:13).

7. **The Local Church and Spiritual Leaders**
   a. Explain differences between local and universal church.
   b. Fellowship with other believers offers spiritual protection, strength, accountability, and oversight from the spiritual leaders the Lord has placed in our lives.
   c. The Bible tells us that "the devil is like a roaring lion seeking to devour us" (1 Peter 5:8). Lions prey on strays, those who are isolated from the herd. That's why we need each other—to protect and encourage us.

**When God Seems Silent**
**Chapter 5 Outline**

# Recognizing His Voice

### 1. A Still, Small Voice

   a.  Elijah discovered that God was not heard in the mighty wind, earthquake and fire, but in a gentle whisper.

   b.  God often speaks quietly by nudging us to obey His voice.

      *Ex: Larry and LaVerne's daughter running through London streets*

   c.  Instead of an earth-shattering way, God usually speaks to us through impressions, thoughts and feelings.

      *Ex: Mark Virkler*

### 2. Recognizing That Inner Voice

   a.  We often believe that hearing God's voice is complicated, but it is really not as hard as we may think.

      *Ex: South Carolina mission work*

   b.  Sometimes God speaks by placing a desire or burden in our hearts that we would not be from anyone else but God.

### 3. What Energizes You?

   a.  Motivational gifts energize us, and God speaks to us through these gifts.

      *Ex: business owner, pastor, missionary, prophet, intercessor, entrepreneur or helping others*

   b.  God generally does not ask us to do something we hate doing, but what we enjoy.

      *Ex: Music, teaching children*

### 4. What Next?

   a.  The more hard-hearted we become, the more difficult it is for us to hear and obey the Lord. If we sin, our heavenly Father wants us to come boldly to His throne and receive forgiveness.

b.  Conviction may come from an inner prompting, reading or hearing the Word of God or other unconventional ways.

   *Ex: Bakery owner awakened from sleep.*

## 5. Failure Is Not Who You Are

a.  What we do with failure can change our course.

   *Ex: Thomas Edison*

   *Ex: Larry as a young man*

   *Ex: John Creasy, novelist*

b.  Bible examples of those who failed but refused to quit.

   *Ex: From Moses to Joshua to Esther to Paul*

## 6. Who are You?

a.  Sometimes we cannot hear God clearly because we feel as if we are not righteous enough. But the truth is that Jesus has made us righteous by faith in Him.

b.  We often "see" with blurred vision. When we have the correct "prescription," we see ourselves as God's children.

   *Ex: Larry and LaVerne's daughter Leticia needing glasses*

## 7. The Unexpected Speaker

a.  God uses the most ordinary things in unexpected ways to speak to us.

   *Ex: Children's Barbie book*

b.  Sometimes He even uses people we least expect to be his mouthpiece to speak to us.

   *Ex: Ungodly king*

c.  Discernment is the key to knowing if you are hearing God's voice through a non-Christian's message. The truth is the same goes for hearing God through a godly person.

   *Ex: Oswald Chambers*

## When God Seems Silent
### Chapter 6 Outline

# Learning to Listen

### 1. Take Time to Listen
    a.  Designate a special time of day to be alone with the Lord.
        *Ex: Marriage relationship*

    b.  Max Lucado writes that some people practice a type of surrogate spirituality, where we rely on others to spend time with God and try to benefit from their experience.
        *Ex: Vacationing*

    c.  Time with God gives us the opportunity to hear Him speak so that we can be encouraged and in turn encourage others.

### 2. Our Time Alone With God
    a.  God whispers so that we will move closer to Him.

    b.  Developing a love relationship with the Lord changes us. We hear His voice more clearly when we spend time in His Word.

    c.  Trying to listen for God's voice but not spending time reading God's Word will open us up to hearing voices that are not from the Lord. Knowing the written Word of God protects us from deception.

    d.  The more listening time you spend with your heavenly Father, the better you will understand His heart for you.
        *Ex: Fast-food drive through.*

### 3. Prayer
    a.  How prayer affects our everyday lives.
        *Ex: Cornell Haan rebellion and mother's reaction*

    b.  God will respond after persistent prayer.
        *Ex: Biblical examples*

    c.  Persevere and continue to ask until we receive the answer.

## 4. Learning to Listen

a. Journaling is writing down your thoughts, prayers, fears, disappointments, joys and miracles.

b. When God speaks, He told Habakkuk to record the vision.

## 5. Fasting

a. When we fast, we starve our bodies in order to feed our spirits.

b. In Mark 9, Jesus said the boy with an evil spirit could only be healed through prayer and fasting.

c. Bible records examples of godly men and women receiving direction from the Lord as a result of fasting.

*Ex: Daniel*

*Ex: Queen Esther*

## 6. Knowing His Character

a. How we see the character of God affects our relationship with Him.

*Ex: Husband and wife relationship*

b. Moses learned to know the character of God; however, the children of Israel only saw the things that God did because they did not have a personal relationship with Him.

c. We know we are hearing God's voice when it matches the character and words of Jesus.

## 7. Check Your Gauges

a. Compare the example of car gauges with spiritual gauges.

b. God has given three specific personal gauges to measure our passion for Jesus and hear His voice clearly.

*Ex: Spirit gauge—time with our heavenly father each day*

*Ex: Soul gauge—our mind, will, and emotions—needs to be cleansed and revitalized regularly*

*Ex: Body gauge—keeping healthy and fit.*

## When God Seems Silent
### Chapter 7 Outline

# Beware of the 12 D's of the Devil

1. **Unmet Expectations and the Silence of God**
   a. The devil tries to destroy us through the process called the 12 D's of the Devil: Disappointment, Discontentment, Discouragement, Doubt, Disbelief, Disillusionment, Deception, Disobedience, Discord, Dysfunction, Despair and Destruction.

   b. If we forgive, release and apply the grace of God to our lives, we will receive freedom. But if we do not forgive, we will fall into the trap of the 12 D's of the devil.

2. **The Twelve D's of the Devil: the Initial Stages**
   a. If we take our broken disappointment to God, He will give us the ability to navigate them.

   *Ex: Rough road illustration*

   b. Why do good people fall into horrible sin? It does not happen overnight, but slowly.

   *Ex: Frog dropped into water that is slowly heated*

   c. Disappointment grows into discontentment and discouragement. Doubt is the danger zone.

3. **The Twelve D's of the Devil: the Process Continues**
   a. The enemy's plan for destruction in your life continues into disbelief or unbelief, which is the final form of doubt. Disillusionment is followed by deception and disobedience.

   b. Don't allow disbelief, disillusionment, deception and disobedience to lead you further from the plans that God has for you.

## 4. The Twelve D's of the Devil: Enemy's Sinister Plan

a. Discord is followed by dysfunction and confusion abounds. Despair causes lose of hope. Destruction is the enemy's final plan: physical, emotional and spiritual death.

b. Refuse to fall for the 12 D's of the devil. God redeems.

## 5. The Bell Theory

a. Even when we forgive, we often continue to deal with the painful memories.

b. Secret to finding freedom from the painful memories.

*Ex: Corrie Ten Boom and the reverberating bell*

*Ex: Woman who had abortions*

## 6. Unfilled Dreams

a. The disciples thought it was all over when Jesus went to the cross, but it was only the beginning! Like the disciples, we find that God often fulfills our unfulfilled dreams in amazing ways that are above what we can imagine.

*Ex: Paul the apostle*

## 7. Beware of the Counterfeit

a. The Bible says that in the last days, many false prophets will rise up and tell people what their ears want to hear.

*Ex: Psychics on TV shows.*

b. The enemy will scheme to keep you from hearing from God and even create a counterfeit.

c. God's voice will be distorted if you place something or someone ahead of Him.

*Ex: Ezekiel (Ezekiel 14:1-5)*

*Ex: Children of Israel demanding quail.*

## When God Seems Silent
### Chapter 8 Outline
# Embracing the Journey

1. **The Dark Night of the Soul**
   a. Jesus cried out in anguish on the cross, "My God, my God, why have you forsaken me?" (Matthew 27:46). This experience sometimes is called the dark night of the soul.
   b. Do not fear the dark night of the soul, because it is a reminder that we need Him desperately and often motivates us to place our full trust in God.
   c. The deepest sorrows and the highest joys are best shared in silence.
   *Ex: Paul Thigpen*
   d. When God is silent, it doesn't mean that He is absent.
   *Ex: Zephaniah, the prophet*
   *Ex: King David*

2. **Consolation and Desolation**
   a. Consolation is when "the soul is inflamed with love for the Lord.
   b. Desolation is darkness of the soul, turmoil of the mind.
   *Ex: Ignatius' focus on "sufficient grace"*
   *(2 Corinthians 12:9,10).*

3. **Surprised by His Voice**
   a. Sometimes God speaks in a way we would never expect.
   *Ex: The Lord speaking through a donkey to Balaam.*
   b. God spoke in audible voice to the prophets and to Paul.
   c. Hear with understanding.
   *Ex: Samuel and Paul*

4. **Touched by an Angel**
   a. God created angels to watch over and assist us.
      *Ex: Psalm 91:11 says, "For he will command his angels concerning you to guard you on all your ways."*
      *Ex: Peter released from prison*
      *Ex: Albanian friend*

5. **Look to See what He Will Say**
   a. "I will look to see what he will say to me" (Habakkuk 2:1).
   b. Be careful not to assume that God will speak to us in only one particular way. Look around and see how He is working and learn to recognize the activity of God.
      *Ex: Husband noticing needs of wife*
      *Ex: Henry Blackaby*

6. **He is the God of the Process**
   a. God's purpose is the process.
      *Ex: Oswald Chambers*
   b. God may be silent due to no fault of our own.
   c. Sin alienates us from God and creates a barrier to hearing.
      *Ex: In the days of Samuel*
      *Ex: King David*
   d. Persevere. God is faithful.
      *Ex: George Mueller*

7. **A Life of Devotion**
   a. We will not hear the Lord's voice clearly if we only listen when He tells us what we want to hear.
   b. Practice living minute by minute in the presence of God.
      *Ex: Brother Lawrence*
   c. God is a good God. Even when He seems to be silent, He is faithful and preparing you for the days ahead. Embrace the journey.

*Reflection journaling space*
Chapter 1 **When God Seems to Stop Speaking**

**DAY 1** *Have you experienced the silence of God? How does God's promise never to forsake you, apply to your situation?*

**DAY 2** *Are you longing to hear God's voice but wavering in faith because you cannot hear God speaking? Describe your circumstances and why you believe God is allowing you to go through this time of silence.*

**DAY 3** *Can you see areas in your life where God may be weeding out your dependence upon others so that you depend more upon Him?*

**DAY 4** *Now is the time to commit your circumstances to God. Write down your commitment and tell God you are willing to obey Him regardless.*

**DAY 5** *Are your circumstances drowning out God's voice? Write down a few scriptures that apply to your situation.*

**DAY 6** *Why must we be careful to discern the voices vying for our attention? What can we trust to be sure that we are truly following God even when we cannot feel His presence?*

**DAY 7** *Have you been tempted to believe that the sun is not shining because your life isn't being blessed in the way you desire? How can you know that God is good and that you are blessed even in the darkest night?*

*Reflection journaling space*
Chapter 2 **Seasons**

**DAY 1** *Describe some past season that seemed hard, but now you see how the Lord was preparing you for the future? Which season do you feel you are in at this time?*

**DAY 2** *Can you remember a time when you needed to endure but moved hastily and missed God's blessing? Is there an area of your life where you need to exercise patience?*

**DAY 3** *Why is it important to give thanks? In what areas do you need the most practice in giving thanks?*

**DAY 4** *Where is your focus when things go wrong? How can you "pop back up" when you feel pushed over?*

**DAY 5** *Give an example of a time that you received bad news? What was your response? How should we respond to the dark night of the soul?*

**DAY 6** *Jesus made three powerful statements. What were they? When did Jesus face the silence of his heavenly Father?*

**DAY 7** *What does it mean to live in the "land in between?" Ask God, "What do you want me to do now"?*

*Reflection journaling space*
Chapter 3 **Taking Baby Steps**

**DAY 1** *Can you think of any baby steps the Lord may be leading you to take in faith? What happens to people who spend their lives in fear of making a mistake?*

**DAY 2** *What is the first step to having a breakthrough in your life? How can we waste our mistakes? What is a scripture to claim when we make a mistake?*

**DAY 3** *Have you detected a pattern of healthy or destructive fear or perhaps lack of fear pertaining to your relationship with the Lord? What can we expect to experience when we walk in the fear of the Lord?*

**DAY 4** *Are you in the midst of chaos? In what ways can you "come apart" to meet God?*

**DAY 5** *Give some examples of when your life was enriched by embracing your God-given responsibility? Are there any areas in your life where you should change your perspective?*

**DAY 6** *Give an example of a spiritual battle with which you have struggled. Explain the sentence: "You cannot have great victories without going through great battles."*

**DAY 7** *What does it mean to you to be a friend of God? Explain the difference between God the Father, God the Son, and God the Holy Spirit.*

*Reflection journaling space*
Chapter 4 **Walking in Faith**

**DAY 1** *Why are words important? Give an example of how speaking truth has set you free? What are some scriptures to help you experience truth during a difficult time?*

**DAY 2** *Can you recall a time in your life where you heard a teaching that did not line up with Scripture? How can God's Word help us discern the voices we hear?*

**DAY 3** *How can you distinguish between condemnation and conviction of the Holy Spirit? Describe a time the Lord spoke to you through conviction.*

**DAY 4** *What are some wrong ways to respond to criticism? What is the proper way to respond to criticism?*

**DAY 5** *Is there something you have learned from history that is shaping your life and walk with Christ today?*

**DAY 6** *Why is a community of believers important in helping you hear from God? Give an example of how the local church has helped you hear the Lord speak.*

**DAY 7** *How does the Lord use spiritual leaders in our lives to help us hear from God?*

*Reflection journaling space*
Chapter 5 **Recognizing His Voice**

**DAY 1** *Has God ever prompted you by an inner nudge that you recognized as His still, small voice? Describe what happened.*

**DAY 2** *Explain how spontaneous thoughts, feelings and impressions can be God's voice. Give an example when the Lord spoke to you with a gentle whisper.*

**DAY 3** *How do you generally hear God speaking? How do you nurture the natural gifts that God gives?*

**DAY 4** *How does conviction stir your conscience to want to know God better? Have you ever ignored the Holy Spirit's conviction and your heart became hardened?*

**DAY 5** *Have you experienced a failure that has discouraged you or caused you to quit trying? What truths can you tell yourself in order to become the conqueror God intends?*

**DAY 6** *How can you apply the truth of being righteous in Christ to your life?*

**DAY 7** *Did God ever give you an unexpected revelation that you knew was His voice speaking personally to you? What is the key to knowing if you are hearing God's voice through a non-Christian?*

*Reflection journaling space*
Chapter 6 **Learning to Listen**

**DAY 1** *Why is it important to take time alone with God every day? How does this personal discipline apply to your life? Do you need to make any changes?*

**DAY 2** *Why is it important to focus on both prayer and the Word of God each day? How do you keep your time with God each day from becoming an obligation?*

**DAY 3** *Why is it important to continue with perseverance in prayer? What spiritual lesson can we learn from Jesus' story in Luke 11?*

**DAY 4** *Describe what journaling is in your own words. Do you record God's activity through journaling?*

**DAY 5** *How do prayer and fasting go hand in hand? Give an example of the Lord speaking to you while fasting.*

**DAY 6** *What does it mean when God says He loves us? How do you know God loves you?*

**DAY 7** *How can you keep your spirit healthy? How can you keep your soul healthy? How can you keep your body healthy?*

*Reflection journaling space*
Chapter 7 **Beware the 12 D's of the Devil**

**DAY 1** *Share an unmet expectation that you have experienced. How can you avoid a root of bitterness?*

**DAY 2** *What is the key scripture that the revelation of the 12 D's of the devil is built on? What must we do to find freedom from the enemy's plan?*

**DAY 3** *Have you found yourself among any of the 12 D's of the devil? How could any of these stages be affecting you from hearing clearly from the Lord?*

**DAY 4** *What is a key to living life to the fullest?*

**DAY 5** *Explain the bell theory. Has there ever been a time when you found it hard to forgive?*

**DAY 6** *In what ways can you shift your focus from dissatisfaction to fulfillment in Him?*

**DAY 7** *What are some counterfeits of the Holy Spirit's work? In what ways have you seen these counterfeits in your own life? What can you do to counter the enemy's deception?*

*Reflection journaling space*
Chapter 8 **Embracing the Journey**

**DAY 1** *What can we learn from King David about experiencing the silence of God? What can we learn from Isaiah about experiencing the silence of God?*

**DAY 2** *What is the difference between consolation and desolation? How do we apply the truth of "sufficient grace" to our lives?*

**DAY 3** *Did God ever speak to you in an unexpected way? Is it possible to hear God speak but not understand what He is saying?*

**DAY 4** *Have you ever experienced an angelic encounter? According to the Bible, what do angels do for us?*

**DAY 5** *Can you give an example of a time when you saw God doing something that spoke to you?*

**DAY 6** *Have I obeyed the last thing the Lord asked me to do? Explain: "God is not working toward a particular fin-ish—His purpose is the process itself."*

**DAY 7** *Name some attributes of friendship. Do you have this type of friendship with God?*

**Read Larry's blog** at www.dcfi.org/blog
**Like** Larry and LaVerne Kreider on Facebook
**Follow** Larry Kreider on Twitter

## Biblical Foundation Series

This series by Larry Kreider covers basic Christian doctrine. Practical illustrations accompany the easy-to-understand format. Use for small group teachings (48 outlines), in mentoring relationship or as a daily devotional. Each book has 64 pages: **$4.99** each, 12 Book Set: **$39**
**Available in Spanish and French.**

**Titles in this series:**

1 **Knowing Jesus Christ as Lord**
2 **The New Way of Living**
3 **New Testament Baptisms**
4 **Building For Eternity**
5 **Living in the Grace of God**
6 **Freedom from the Curse**
7 **Learning to Fellowship with God**
8 **What is the Church?**
9 **Authority and Accountability**
10 **God's Perspective on Finances**
11 **Called to Minister**
12 **The Great Commission**

## The Cry for Spiritual Mothers and Fathers

Returning to the biblical truth of spiritual parenting is necessary so believers are not left fatherless and disconnected. How loving, seasoned spiritual fathers and mothers help spiritual children reach their full potential in Christ. *by Larry Kreider, 224 pages*: $14.99

## Your Personal House of Prayer

Christians often struggle with their prayer lives. With the unique "house plan" developed in this book, each room corresponding to a part of the Lord's Prayer, your prayer life is destined to go from duty to joy!

Includes a helpful Daily Prayer Guide to use each day. *by Larry Kreider, 192 pages:* $12.99